Australia's Catholics Today

LOST!

MICHAEL GILCHRIST

First published in 2006 by
Freedom Publishing Company Pty Ltd
582 Queensberry Street
North Melbourne
Victoria 3051
Australia

Printed by
Brougham Press
33 Scoresby Road
Bayswater
Victoria 3153
Australia

ISBN: 0-9775699-1-8

CONTENTS

Acknowledgement: I wish to thank those many people who have contributed generously to the present book via materials, proof-reading, suggestions and corrections.

AUSTRALIA'S CATHOLIC DIOCESES

Introduction

"Lost", as used in the Scriptures, can refer to "lost sheep" or "sheep without a shepherd", in other words today's unchurched Catholics who comprise the vast majority in contemporary Australia, as in other parts of the Western world. It can mean spiritually impoverished, as most of the graduates of the Catholic education system have become since the 1970s. It can point to the loss of identity in many dioceses and Church institutions as well as to those who have "lost the plot" in opting for New Age spiritualities, pantheistic nature worship or radical feminism.

In these and other senses most members of the Catholic Church in Australia are "lost".

Pope Benedict XVI seems to share this assessment, for during a question and answer session in July 2005 with the bishop and priests of

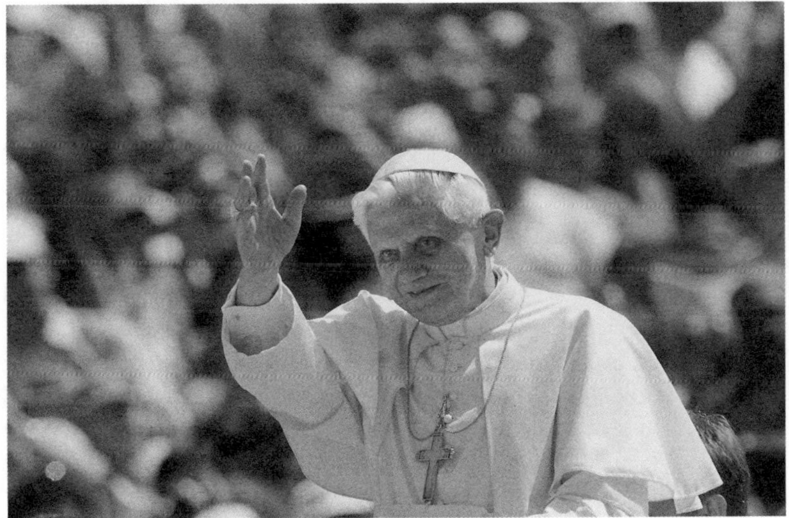

Pope Benedict XVI

the Diocese of Aosta in northern Italy, he referred to the loss of faith in the Western world. He said, "The mainline Churches appear to be dying. This is true above all in Australia and also in Europe, but not so much in the United States ... The Catholic Church is not in such bad shape as the historical mainline Protestant Churches, but it also faces the problems of this moment in history".[1]

While the Catholic Church in Australia may not yet be on its last legs as some Protestant Churches are, its overall condition gives cause for serious concern as it enters its third century, following the first European settlement of New South Wales in 1788. Benedict's words "above all in Australia" prompt one to ask whether the Church in this country can survive as a whole in any meaningfully Catholic sense beyond the 21st century — as distinct from a collection of faithful remnants.

This question is important, not just for Catholics, but for all people of good will, since the Catholic Church is the largest and most cohesive religious body in Australia. If it collapses or is further weakened, there will be little of religious substance left to offset the inroads of secularism to which the other mainline Christian denominations have largely capitulated.

At the best of times, Christianity faces a challenge of survival in one of the world's most secularised nations, but especially so since the fallout from the cultural upheaval of the late 1960s.

It was this situation which prompted the late Mr B.A. Santamaria to found *AD2000* as a monthly journal of religious opinion in 1988, with the aim of promoting and defending Christian and Catholic orthodoxy which has been under attack from inside and outside the Church.

After 18 years as assistant editor and later editor following Mr Santamaria's death in 1998, I am consolidating my thoughts on the state of the contemporary Church in Australia in order to encourage further debate on the best means of ensuring its future survival and even recovery.

While I lay no claim to specialist qualifications in such areas of learning as theology, liturgy or Scripture, as an educated Catholic I have been in a strategic position over an extended period to observe a wide variety of developments and events in the Church throughout Australia and around the world. In doing so, I have assimilated large quantities of material covering every aspect of Church life, including papal encyclicals, Vatican documents, diocesan publications, research findings on belief and practice, and documented nonsense or dissent masquerading as renewal.

Since 1989, many hundreds of Catholics from around the country have contacted me (often with documentation) about situations — positive and negative — occurring in their parishes, schools and dioceses. I have also had on-going contacts with a number of Australian bishops.

I have travelled widely on lecture tours, meeting people in troubled dioceses around Australia, as well as overseas where comparisons could be made with the Australian situation.

Our office — the Thomas More Centre — has hosted many prominent people connected with the Church, from Australia and overseas, and they have given informative addresses and briefings.

Prior to accepting Mr Santamaria's invitation to become assistant editor of *AD2000* at the start of 1989, I had spent close to 30 years of my working life in Catholic education, encompassing all secondary school levels in various Melbourne colleges, including stints as a year 12 Victorian examiner.

Later, I lectured at Catholic institutes of teacher education in Melbourne and Ballarat which subsequently became campuses of Australian Catholic University (ACU). The problems afflicting parts of ACU today were evident during my time at these campuses in the 1970s and 1980s.

I participated in interview panels for prospective student teachers during that period. These young people were mostly products of the Catholic education system and, even at that time, its deficiencies were apparent during many of the interviews where knowledge of the faith was negligible despite up to 12 years attendance at Catholic schools.

Teacher education duties also involved my visiting scores of Catholic primary and secondary schools across Melbourne and country Victoria in order to observe hundreds of lessons given by student teachers, many of them on religious topics. The content of these underlined how doctrinally shallow were the officially sanctioned programs and guidelines.

During the latter part of my career in teacher education, I was prompted to put pen to paper on the state of the Church. The resultant books — *Rome or the Bush* (1986) and *New Church, or True Church* (1987) — drew predictably irate responses from some in high places, although the reactions of grass roots Catholics were more of relief or gratitude that someone had written in depth about the real condition of the Church in Australia after years of official denial.[2]

The present book comes 20 years after the launch of *Rome or the Bush*, which occurred at the time of John Paul II's first visit to Australia. Attending one of his appearances in Melbourne, in connection with Catholic education, I was impressed by the Pope's dynamism and charisma, and was filled with hope about the Church's future under such a strong leader.

My research for the above books had made me belatedly aware of what was occurring under the banner of "renewal", including defective, misguided programs and practices in such areas as liturgy, religious education, seminary formation and spirituality that merely worsened an already obvious crisis of faith. But I was optimistic John Paul II's formidable leadership would soon have a beneficial impact, bringing some order and clarity to the Church and her teachings and disciplines.

Twenty years on, despite John Paul II's long pontificate and the advent of solidly Catholic bishops like Cardinal George Pell, Archbishop Barry Hickey and others since the 1990s (see Chapter 9), the decline has continued, serving to underline how deep-seated are the Church's problems.

This book assumes readers have at least a rudimentary knowledge of the Catholic Church, its hierarchical structure, doctrinal and moral teachings, disciplines, sacraments and liturgy. The frequently used word "orthodox" ("orthodoxy") refers to an unqualified acceptance of these as determined by the Pope and bishops in union with him. These are set out in authoritative documents such as the *Catechism of the Catholic Church* and papal encyclicals.

The parlous condition of Catholicism in Australia means that the strengthening of orthodoxy must be the number one priority if the Church is to survive with its identity intact. It has to be counter-cultural in the midst of secularism, resisting the soft options of accommodation and relevance. Theological adventurism and liturgical experimentation are luxuries the Church can do without in the present circumstances.

Moreover, a commitment to orthodoxy is the only approach that will attract any of the young on a long term basis, as evidenced in the upswing in vocations reflected in seminary enrolments (see chapter 10) and the focus of the more successful ecclesial movements and communities that have emerged in recent decades.

However, for much of the time since the Second Vatican Council (1962-1965), Catholicism in Australia has been shaped by well-placed decision-makers seeking a "creative" implementation of the Council's documents, often at odds with their actual content. Where the documents are silent or vague, the "spirit of Vatican II" is confidently invoked.

What has happened within the Church since the late 1960s mirrors trends in the wider society. Emasculated religion programs, sacraments and liturgies have had parallels in the dumbing down of secular subjects like maths, language, history and music. It was not a good time for the Church to be receptive to the trends and mind-sets of the contemporary world.

The steady decline in belief and practice among Australia's Catholics no doubt has had many contributing causes, some of them beyond the Church's direct control. But those who have held the reins over this period deserve to be held accountable — as would be the case in any other failed enterprise, be it in sport, government or big business.

This is not to impugn the sincerity of such individuals. Many of them no doubt believe today's Australian Catholics cannot or will not accept "difficult" moral or spiritual directives. The only "realistic" approach is to keep lowering the bar — otherwise more of the flock will vote with their feet. But in fact years of such accommodation and overall confusion have contributed to the continuing exodus.

The subjects covered and cases cited in this short book are but a few of the many to hand. Subjects not given in-depth treatment, such as the corruption and disintegration of much of religious life, the inroads of radical feminism through bodies like Women and the Australian Church, the extent to which pantheistic nature worship and neo-paganism have infected Church organisations, the decline of the Catholic hospital system, or, on a positive note, the Church's many new movements and successful religious communities, could have been given separate chapters. Likewise, many more problem dioceses warranted detailed treatment, but I have confined myself to a few of the more striking examples.

What is covered is a rough cross-section of the state of Catholicism around Australia. Enough is said to make points without labouring them and testing readers' endurance with endless illustrations.

Some may consider much of this book to be overly negative or pessimistic. However, I defy anyone to put a positive spin on the present statistics and trends — all of them the results of professionally conducted research. The stark reality — however unpalatable — has first to be grasped if there is to be any turning of the tide. The facts speak for themselves.

Few Australian Catholics have a comprehensive view of the real state of their Church, since what has occurred over the past 30 or more years has been fairly gradual. The declining minority that still practise the faith tend to view the position in their own parish, school or organisation — for better or worse — as "normal". They are usually unaware of the bigger picture since few of them read religious periodicals or books that might keep them in touch with developments in the wider Church. The little religious information they assimilate tends to come from superficial or biased reports in the secular media.

While the earlier chapters of this book concentrate on the weakened condition of parts of today's Church in Australia, the later chapters strike a more hopeful note, focusing on some of the positive developments already occurring while advancing a few suggestions for addressing the present difficulties.

Of course, the hidden actions of God's grace can never be evaluated statistically, and it is in grace that our salvation — and that of our country — lies. We are not in a position to know what the Almighty is working and preparing in Australian hearts and minds, here and now. But what we can see and evaluate gives ample cause for alarm and we need, humanly speaking, to do what is in the realm of the possible.

Endnotes

1. *L'Osservatore Romano*, Italian edition, 27 July 2005.
2. Gilchrist, M.T., *Rome or the Bush*, John XXIII Fellowship Co-op, Ltd, Melbourne, 1986; *New Church or True Church*, John XXIII Fellowship Co-op, Melbourne, 1987.

Chapter One

The Challenge

What, if anything, can be done in the short term to halt or even reverse the negative trends in belief and practice, as noted by Benedict XVI in his comments on the Western world's crisis of faith, "above all in Australia"?

Such a question might seem mystifying to those in the many small pockets of devout Catholicism one still finds around Australia; even more so to those engaged in preparations for the 2008 World Youth Day in Sydney which one hopes will spark a national spiritual revival.

This question does not indicate a lack of awareness of positive developments and happenings, but it considers the broader picture of the Church in Australia, a Church that 50 years ago was one of the masses, rather than of a series of enthusiastic, committed remnants.

These remnants may well provide a basis for fruitful re-growth in the future, but when one examines the condition of the Church as a whole, the picture today looks decidedly bleak and is worsening with each passing year as the statistical evidence makes abundantly clear.

Meanwhile, many of the Church's leaders remain either in denial or damage control mode, or even make a virtue out of necessity, with some liberals convinced the present situation is the work of the Holy Spirit, or at least the fourth member of the Trinity, the "spirit of

Vatican II".

In contrast, Benedict XVI has a much clearer understanding of the real situation in countries like Australia and what is needed to address it.

Archbishop Michael Miller, Secretary of the Vatican Congregation for Catholic Education, offered an analysis of Benedict's thinking in this regard during a speech on 31 October 2005 at Notre Dame University, Indiana, as reported in the *Notre Dame University Observer*.

Archbishop Miller based his analysis on the writings of Cardinal Joseph Ratzinger, now Pope. He said the writings indicate that Benedict believes it is a mistake to uphold institutions that lack a solid Catholic identity.

"[He has] argued that it might be better for the Church not to expend its resources trying to preserve institutions if their Catholic identity has been seriously compromised," the Archbishop said. "His writings show that a time of purification lies ahead, and this undoubtedly will have some ramifications for Catholic institutions".

Archbishop Miller added that the Pope believes the "measure of an institution can be judged by its Catholic integrity" and that "if a Catholic institution is no longer motivated by a Catholic identity, it is better to let it go".

Orthodox remnants aside, many of the Church's structures in Australia have lost their Catholic identity — the taste of their "salt" (Matt 5:13).

While the general thrust of the Church's operations in many dioceses, schools and parishes seems attuned to a lowest common denominator version of the faith — a spiritual comfort zone — a continuation of this approach can only ensure further spiritual erosion. Better, as Benedict suggests, to focus primarily on those parts of the Church that are capable of maintaining their Catholic identity and have prospects of growth. The other sectors that appear to be beyond salvaging — as is sadly the case with some of the major religious orders — should be jettisoned or allowed to wither on the vine, rather than continue to weaken the faith of the orthodox remnants.

John Paul II

The Australian situation is similar to that existing in much of the Western world, notably Europe, North America and New Zealand, where the inroads of the late 1960s cultural revolution and its accompanying secularism and relativism found many Church leaders ill-prepared and confused following the heady days of Vatican II and its aftermath when many in high places were calling for radical changes to the Church's doctrines, disciplines, liturgy — indeed, to just about everything.

The worst crime for any Catholic was to be "pre-Vatican II", to even think of questioning the feverish obsession with change at all costs. The Council, after all, was seen by many as a new Pentecost, a time for fresh beginnings. That kind of thinking survives to this day among the ageing band of Church revolutionaries and their like-minded successors who continue to run parts of the Church.

Pope John Paul II addresses Australia's bishops during the Synod of Oceania in 1998

When Pope John Paul II first visited Australia in November 1986, many Catholics hoped that genuine renewal of the Church was on the horizon thanks to the powerful, charismatic leadership of this remarkable Pope following his election in 1978.

At that time, the "spirit of Vatican II" decision-makers continued to determine the thinking of many Catholic education offices, liturgy bodies, religious orders, seminaries, departments of theology and teacher-training institutes — with the disastrous results for the Church so plain to see today.

But it was hoped the ineffectual bishops who had presided over the spiritual decline in the aftermath of Vatican II would in due course be replaced by a new generation of stronger, no-nonsense, "John Paul II bishops" who would put the architects of failure on notice.

The leadership style prevalent after the Council had involved rejection of the pre-Vatican II past, an openness to change, an informality and a reluctance to uphold or impose orthodoxy if this involved any boat-rocking. These bishops (including some "born again" older bishops) saved their rare exercises of authority for keeping the Church's unhappy conservatives or traditionalists under control. There were a few exceptions to this pattern, such as Bishop Bernard Stewart of Sandhurst (who retired in 1979). But such bishops were swimming against the tide.

In books such as Paul Johnson's *Pope John Paul II and the Catholic Restoration* (1981), there was anticipation of a Catholic recovery fuelled by John Paul's succession of inspiring encyclicals and other written statements that, among other things, pinpointed the spiritual trouble-spots and what needed to be done, and his stirring personal appearances before millions throughout the world.

However, as we move into the Church's third millennium (or third century in Australia), that optimism has dissipated as the downward slide continues unabated. The church bureaucrats (or their like-minded successors) who presided over the decline retain their influence while relatively few bishops seem disposed to tackle the crisis of faith with effective strategies. Those who attempt to are often attacked or undermined from inside or outside the Church.

Administrative breakdown

Herein lies the core of the problem: a fundamental breakdown in administration, from the Vatican down to parish and school levels. Since catholic means universal, there can be no "Australian Church". The Church in Australia needs to be in harmony with the universal Church.

Throughout his long pontificate up to his death in April 2005, John Paul II issued numerous encyclicals and apostolic letters, but many of them have remained dead-letters, consigned to the too-hard-basket in many Australian dioceses.

At the same time, "leading" theologians, self-proclaimed experts and media commentators have publicly rejected or contested some of the papal documents, using the secular media as their vehicle, with John Paul disparaged as out of touch with the needs of the Church in progressive Western nations like Australia. Bishops aligning themselves with the Papal agenda have been labelled as reactionaries by those seeing their long-occupied spheres of influence under threat.

In truth it is the papal critics who are the real reactionaries today, trapped as they are in their 60s and 70s time warp and spiritual blinkers. Some of them even now remain convinced that further doses of the same failed policies are the key to solving the Church's problems.

This has been highlighted over the past 20 years with many dioceses launching ambitious programs on the pattern of the discredited "Renew" — widely used in Australia during the 1980s — with trendy labels like "Tomorrow's Church", "Creating Our Future", "Never Ending Story", "Building Our Future Together", "A Time for Listening" and "Call to Change", along with predictions of imminent new Pentecosts.

On the whole, despite the vast expenditures of time, money and human resources, these have left behind little of spiritual value. They are now mostly forgotten, save by a few "empowered" liberal-minded activists, keen to exercise more influence in priestless — and increasingly parishioner-less — parishes.

Today, most Catholics remain only vaguely aware of such developments. Apathetic on religious issues and ill-informed on the faith, they are basically indistinguishable in their moral values and behaviour from the rest of the community, and impervious to any teachings from the Pope or bishops. It is no wonder such anti-Christian books as Dan Brown's *The Da Vinci Code* have proved to be so popular, even among Catholics. For many, such books are often their first introduction to Church history.

Other Catholics, including some members of well-known religious orders, have sought to fill the spiritual vacuum with New Age superstitions, radical feminism or trendy political causes.

(New Age is an umbrella term which encompasses faith in the power of crystals, worship of the natural environment, aspects of Buddhism and Hinduism, self-improvement programs like the Enneagram, and elements of primitive and pre-Christian religions. Many so-called spirituality programs offered in parishes and schools contain some of these New Age ingredients).

Causes of malaise

Since the 1970s there has been a steady decline in the numbers of Catholics knowing, believing or practising what the Church teaches. This trend shows no sign of levelling out.

One can debate the causes of the malaise. No doubt they include the almost suffocating influences of secularism, materialism and relativism — especially via the media and entertainment industries — along with weakened family and moral life. But inept or misguided Church leadership and policy-making at the local level have made a difficult situation worse.

The loss of identity and subsequent disintegration of the larger religious orders which formerly ran the Church's schools with selfless dedication for a century have contributed to the general falling-away, whilst the introduction of government funding for non-state schools since the 1960s has removed one of the factors which solidified Catholics through their century-long struggle for justice, and united parish communities in common sacrifices to build and maintain their schools.

Spiritually and morally bankrupt secularism may eventually run out of steam, but the Church cannot afford to wait it out before putting its house in order. Otherwise there will be little left with which to fill the vacuum.

If current trends are allowed to continue, the Church in Australia will soon become little more than an empty shell of cathedrals, churches, convents and schools populated by small enclaves of practising remnants now shrunken to barely five per cent of the Catholic population — with the balance being Catholic in name only.

As with other failing mainline denominations, the Church will retain its existence as an historical or cultural entity, serving as an occasional port of call for weddings, funerals, concerts and ceremonial occasions where the numbers are often misleadingly impressive.

Impossible dream

For any early broad-based recovery, there would need to be — an impossible dream — the almost overnight appointments of 20 to 30 strong, courageous, solidly orthodox bishops, with a clear understanding of the situation, a well thought out agenda and a fearless determination to see it through whatever the obstacles.

To this would need to be added overnight several hundred soundly formed young priests to staff parishes and visit homes and schools, along with a similar number of religious men and women to reactivate the Catholic education system so that it teaches the truths of faith without equivocation.

True, these kinds of positive developments have been occurring in a piecemeal fashion — as this book shows — and they offer the only realistic basis for limited gains down the track.

Around the world, numerous ecclesial movements and communities, such as Focolare, the Neocatechumenate, Communion and Liberation, Regnum Christi, San Egidio, the Catholic charismatic renewal, the Chemin Neuf, Emmanuel, L'Arche, and Christian Life communities have been consolidating numbers of committed Catholics.

Many of these sprang up after Vatican II in response to the Council's call for the laity to be more active in spreading the Gospel and some of them have put down roots in Australia.

Other concentrations of practising Catholics include Latin Mass communities, home schoolers, pro-lifers, viewers of EWTN (Eternal Word Television Network), and organised bodies of university students, professionals and other like-minded orthodox, although collectively these represent a small portion of the total Catholic population.

Recent trends in most of Australia's seminaries — with the glaring exception of Queensland — have been encouraging, if not dramatic, with a steady trickle of young, orthodox priests entering parish life in some dioceses where reforms have taken place. But most of today's active diocesan and religious clergy were formed during the confusing period of the radicalised seminaries from the late 1960s onwards. Many of them are set in their liturgical or theological ways and with the growing shortfall of available priests, it becomes ever more difficult for even the strongest bishops to read the riot act when abuses or dissent occur.

Selection of bishops

While appointments of bishops to Australia's largest dioceses have been generally encouraging since the early 1990s, and have led to some positive initiatives, the majority of bishops on the Episcopal Conference appear to be in the post-Vatican II "pastoral" mould, averse to any boat-rocking or tough decision-making, while some of them remain a part of the problem.

The prospect of united action by Australia's bishops in the immediate future, say, in regard to implementing *Ex Corde Ecclesiae* (John Paul II's 1990 document calling for religious orthodoxy at Catholic universities), continues to be remote.

This situation underlines the fact that the process of selecting bishops has been significantly flawed, however fail-safe it may appear on paper.

Even during the long pontificate of John Paul II many ineffectual appointments were made to Australian dioceses — men either unable or unwilling to grasp the nettle of serious reform, however devout they might be in their personal lives.

The settled view among these bishops, along with their bureaucrats, clergy, religious and assorted minders, appears to be that a watered-down, cafeteria-style "lite" Catholicism is a fact of life. Lowering the bar is regarded as the way forward and challenging this would merely make matters worse, driving away those few who still attend Mass.

They may have a point, as most Catholics, including regular Mass-attenders, have become so secularised, ignorant of the faith, and acclimatised to a dumbed-down, soft-option Catholicism that they may well desert in droves if suddenly confronted with what the Church actually demands of its membership. The shock could be too great.

To challenge this line can be more than politically incorrect, it can actually put at risk one's position or livelihood. Priests or teachers who present the Church's position in too clear terms for the tastes of many of today's Catholics can expect to be challenged in their parishes or schools, with little official backing in the event of conflict or complaints. Better to stick to safe, popular subjects like global warming, the environment, aboriginal land rights, the "stolen generation", or inclusive, inoffensive Scripture readings.

This approach has perpetuated the trend in many parishes and schools towards a token, accommodating faith that makes few spiritual demands. The effective disappearance of fasting and abstinence and holy days of obligation has aggravated this trend. The longer it continues, the harder it becomes for even the strongest bishops to have much impact on the problem.

But the appointment of such bishops, even to the small suffragan dioceses, remains of major importance, not only for the sake of these dioceses' spiritual welfare, but also for building up the numbers of like-minded bishops on the episcopal conference who are prepared to unite on matters requiring tough decisions and concerted action.

With a fearlessly Catholic bishop in place, young men contemplating the priesthood are more likely to remain in their diocese, rather than gravitate to more orthodox ones. Moreover, in smaller, more manageable dioceses, strong bishops are better placed to have an immediate impact through a direct, hands-on approach.

This was highlighted recently with the appointment of Bishop Robert Finn to the relatively small (145,000 Catholics) US Diocese of Kansas City-St Joseph, Missouri, in 2005. In the 18 months since then he has had an extraordinary impact on every area of church life, including doubled numbers at the seminary. More bishops should emulate his single-minded, courageous leadership.

In the bigger dioceses, even the best efforts of bishops can be blunted or filtered out by the large bureaucracies and institutions they inherit.

Australia's bishops, and those involved in the selection of future bishops, need to ask themselves whether the present trends are acceptable or inevitable. Meanwhile, further documents from the Holy See on doctrines or liturgy will serve little purpose if the bishops 20,000 kilometres away are unable or unwilling to give them force in their dioceses.

Whether the 21st century proves to be the Church in Australia's final or finest hour remains to be seen. Whether it has the will to be pulled back from the brink during the coming decades — short of Divine intervention — is the focus of this book.

Chapter Two

"Spirit of Vatican II" or "new ways of being Church"

The Catholic Church's worsening crisis of faith in Australia has prompted a variety of responses.

The logical approach in the circumstances was a return to basics — for starters, more doctrinal content in parish programs and school curricula, reform of the seminaries, a curbing of liturgical abuses, encouragment of Eucharistic devotions and the provision of in-services for teachers, priests and religious on John Paul II's encyclicals.

Many Australian dioceses, though, preferred instead to mount ambitious, expensive schemes with catchy titles and invitations to open-ended speculation.

Their aim seemed to be — with the shortfall of priests the usual catalyst — a "new model of Church" with extensive restructurings and

Second Vatican Council (1962-1965)

changed roles based on imaginative re-interpretations of Vatican II, provided all this was subjected to a nebulous vision of "Australian culture".

What had occurred since the 1960s in many religious orders, seminaries, Catholic education offices and theology institutes — in the "spirit (or perhaps poltergeist) of Vatican II" — was to be force fed to the practising remnants of the Catholic population.

The new comfort zone

The following are just a few examples of what has been occurring in many dioceses post Vatican II. All presupposed some radical changes in structures, roles and even Church teachings. While this approach has seen the empowerment of local activists, the net spiritual results have been all but invisible, as indicated by the ever emptier pews and drying up of priestly and religious vocations.

The year 1989 alone witnessed numerous "renewal" projects underway across the country as these brief snapshots indicate.

A proposal for lay ministries in the Parramatta Diocese dared to state confidently, "The Catholic Church in general and the local church in particular are in transition from a hierarchical to a community model". In Ballarat, a working document for the Priests' Assembly stated, "We have had a rigid scaffold around us from the past; now is the time to let go and let the tree grow on its own". In Perth, material for a "Year of Mission" Assembly referred to the "need to move away from authoritarian Church structures". The first draft Position Papers for the Canberra-Goulburn Diocesan Synod preferred the "we are church" model to the hierarchical one.[1]

Changes in Church teachings and disciplines were also anticipated with the various gatherings' affirmative votes seen as sending a clear message to Rome.

In Ballarat, draft discussion material for the Priests' Assembly asked whether celibacy was "outmoded and life-denying" and whether more priests were indeed "necessary".

In Brisbane, despite acknowledging Rome still had the final word, a questionnaire for the Archdiocesan Assembly wanted to know the numbers favouring "the introduction of women priests".

While calls at these various assemblies for more "adult education" in the faith seemed on the surface reasonable, it appeared this was subject to a specific interpretation of the faith. In the Parramatta Diocese, "current theological writings" were recommended in connection with lay "leadership", while the Ballarat Priests' Assembly material recommended "competent Catholics be invited to provide information about contemporary Ecclesiology". In Canberra-Goulburn it was asked, "What kind of education/renewal do people most need to prepare them for the changing Church?"[2]

Adelaide

This pattern continued throughout the 1990s in a large number of Australian dioceses, with Melbourne's *Tomorrow's Church* project one of the most ambitious, although by 1996 it would be mercifully put down following the appointment of Archbishop George Pell.

The general view with all such exercises seemed to be that the Church's spiritual health could be gauged, not so much by Mass attendances, confessions, knowledge of the faith, or priestly and religious vocations, but by the number of discussion groups, working parties, position papers, listening sessions, mission statements and assorted gatherings that could be generated in order to reinvent the spiritual wheel.[3]

Adelaide, since the holding of a Diocesan Assembly in 1985, had been a hive of activity in this regard with much talk of "listening", "empowerment", "participation", "equality", "inclusiveness", "local church" and "community." More and more bureaucratic bodies sprang into life to implement reforms, even as numbers declined in the pews and at the seminary. There was much use of churchspeak, intelligible only to the chosen few managing the process.

The May/June 1996 newsletter of the Adelaide *A Time for Listening* project revealed that the Adelaide Diocesan Assembly Working Party had been commissioned by Archbishop Leonard Faulkner at the end of 1994 and met throughout 1995. They had "reflected" on the "diocesan vision, *Community for the World*, the diocesan strategy of Basic Ecclesial Communities and the Pastoral Principles that underpin all this".

Throughout 1995, said the report, "the Working Party — in conversation with the Diocesan Pastoral Team, the Diocesan Pastoral Council and the Council of Priests — began to develop processes to help parishes and other pastoral units to connect with the wider Catholic community and consult with it." In addition, "The Diocesan Assembly was developing into a year of consultation."

The Working Party, had then "consulted and listened to parish priests, ethnic community chaplains, pastoral associates, parish pastoral councils and Catholic school principals". This had led to the consultative process for the Diocesan Assembly titled *A Time for Listening* — "an invitation to the whole diocese to listen to one another ... to reflect on what it means to us to be Catholic in today's world" and "for all in the wider Catholic community to have their say".

A voluminous collection of opinions was published under the heading "Diocesan Assembly '96: Small Group Recommendations to the Church at Parish Community Level."

Among the over 250 recommendations, the following were fairly typical:

"New style of leadership which empowers people".

"We, as people, need to consistently be knocking at the door of the hierarchy. To respond to needs of divorced, to give priests an option to marry. To bring back the priests who are married".

"Work within the system — only a matter of time before the laity emerge as leaders of the Church at the local level".

"Follow-up, inclusivity, communication, empowerment, outreach, challenge".

"Opportunities for our pastors to 'refresh' and to change with the times".

"Educate our people to a new way of thinking".

"Liturgical education reform".

"Empower people to own or live their faith — Basic Ecclesial Communities?"

"Writing Eucharistic Prayers in more simple, meaningful language. Balance between 'being-in-touch' language and 'reverent' language".

"Less sacramental Church more social justice".

In October 1996 the Adelaide Diocesan Assembly, consisting of about 400 representatives from parishes, schools and other organisations endorsed the establishment of Basic Ecclesial Communities. These would be small groups of activist lay Catholics within parishes similar to what had been occurring in Brazil in the absence of priests.

The Pastoral Planning Co-ordinator for the Archdiocese explained that "the aim of the assembly was to listen to the stories of church members and see what they were wanting from the Church. No one part of the Church has all the answers so we have to listen to each other."

This was to be the prevailing pattern in Adelaide until the arrival of a new Archbishop in 2001.

Brisbane

Like Adelaide, most Queensland dioceses had been intoxicated by the "spirit of Vatican II" since the 1960s, with Brisbane taking the lead and its seminary giving impetus to radical thinking throughout the State.

The Brisbane Archdiocese's draft guidelines for the appointment of parish pastoral ministers (i.e., pastoral ministry coordinators, pastoral associates and pastoral directors) were circulated in 1997 by the Executive Director of the Office of Church Life and Mission.

The document set in place what was basically a blueprint for an increasingly lay-run Church, while ensuring the right kinds of people were recruited, namely, those with "a commitment to the Mission and Directions of the Archdiocese of Brisbane".

At the same time, a pair of booklets titled *Celebrate* and *Learn* were published by the Offices of Adult Education and Parish Review and Planning within the office of Brisbane Catholic Education. They each carried the general banner of "Evaluation of Ministry and Service" and were the fruits of the Brisbane Archdiocese's *Shaping Our Future* modernisation and re-structuring blueprint, finalised in 1989.[4]

Each of the booklets called for the setting up of parish "taskforces", with instructions on how these were to evaluate their parish's liturgy and theology. Relevance and political correctness seemed to be the major criteria.

Bureaucratic positions with high-sounding churchspeak titles continued to proliferate, with advertisements in the Brisbane *Catholic Leader* calling for applications for an "Executive Secretary/Project Officer to the Archbishop's Taskgroup on Women's Participation in the Church" and for the post of "Administration/Project Officer within the Vicariate of Church Life and Mission" — the latter requiring applicants have "an understanding of the Mission and Directions of the Archdiocese."[5]

The nature of "Mission and Directions" could be deduced from samples of the 80 plus criteria listed for evaluation by each parish task-force. At the end of each sub-section in the two booklets, the task-force was asked to record its "Assessment" of the parish, whether it was "On the Slide," "In the Pits", "On the Improve" or "Zooming Along."

The *Celebrate* booklet, which concentrated on liturgy, included the following qualities needed to be a "Zooming Along" parish:

"The liturgy planning group ensures it is in touch with current liturgical documents and Archdiocesan guidelines.

"There is a well-constructed, designed and decorated liturgical space for suitable celebrations of the rites of the Church, (e.g., a font for immersion, a eucharistic chapel, seating around the leadership space, a gathering space, etc.)

"Rituals (using movement, symbols, art, drama, etc) are used appropriately to express the connection between God's Word and our everyday life.

"The experience of community takes different forms and reflects different parish styles with different groups in the parish, (e.g., women, single adults, young people, people with disabilities, the elderly, etc.)

"The words and symbols of the liturgy are experienced as being intimately related to everyday life and not as being apart from or irrelevant to it.

"The variety of prayer experiences provided in the parish encompasses the diversity of Catholic traditions of spirituality, particularly a spirituality that deals with the reality of the everyday, the here-and-now."

The *Learn* booklet focused on how to evaluate a parish's theological credentials:

"The parish assists the community's search for God's Spirit in the 'signs of the times,' by keeping abreast in such areas as: the expanding role of the non-ordained in the church and the implications for ministry and mission in that; the search for a contemporary 'spirituality' that is set in the reality of the everyday; processes for social analysis that help to identify God's saving action in the world about us.

"Parishes ensure that they receive regular updates of resources and opportunities available from the various Archdiocesan agencies involved in faith education.

"The spirit and practice of discernment is fostered in the parish. People are encouraged to recognise God's presence and abiding love in key moments of their life, even those where God may seem absent."

No doubt the Jubilee Celebration Liturgy for primary school pupils on 2 August 2000 in St Stephen's Cathedral, Brisbane, would have scored an effortless "Zooming along" rating for its creativity.[6]

An interlude following the Gospel involved depiction of the aboriginal Rainbow Serpent, to the accompaniment of didgeridoo and aboriginal dancers.

A reader first informed the school children that "an important story to the indigenous people of Australia is the story of the Rainbow Serpent. It is a story of the creator spirit." According to this story, "far off in the dreamtime there were no people, no animals or birds, no trees or bushes, no hills or mountains. The country was all flat. The great Rainbow Serpent stirred from the land and set off to create ... With the Rainbow Serpent came life and this life is the life of all people."

As a didgeridoo played, school children carried rainbow stoles "in a serpentine fashion along the centre aisle" of the Cathedral and onto the sanctuary. Aboriginal dancers then stood in a line on the sanctuary holding up the Rainbow Serpent, which was then divided into six rainbow scarves to be worn by a succession of "storytellers."

In 2003 the Pontifical Council for Interreligious Dialogue released a document, *Jesus Christ, the Water Bearer of Life: A Christian Reflection on the New Age*, which warned Catholics against being deceived by attempts to blend Catholicism with other spiritual systems.

But like other such authoritative documents it would gather dust.

Toowoomba

Since the appointment of Bishop William Morris in 1992, the Queensland Diocese of Toowoomba has been catching up with the rest of the

Sunshine State's love affair with the "spirit of Vatican II". This was typified in 2000 by a blueprint for the diocese titled *Creating Our Future*, which contained little if anything that addressed the myriad spiritual problems and inroads of secularism on the faithful.[7]

No doubt considerable time, effort and finance are devoted to such enterprises. As the Chairperson of the Toowoomba Diocesan Pastoral Council explained in her introduction, "Many hours of listening, reflecting, consulting, praying and discussing have gone into making this document. From the Gatherings of 1998 through the work of the Interim Committee and now the Diocesan Pastoral Council itself this year".

The contents of *Creating Our Future* followed the familiar pattern of other unsuccessful, now largely forgotten, renewal projects, with the document's bureaucratic churchspeak more likely to mystify than motivate the faithful, e.g., "The Vision, Mission and Key Pastoral Direction Statement has been birthed from the Diocesan gathering", and "Develop a sense of Diocesan ownership, spirit and connectedness."

A heading, "Key Pastoral Directions," contained the curious subheading, "Through baptism we are called to live out God's dream by ... Developing and updating faith education and spirituality ... Promoting and celebrating life-giving liturgy ... Exploring various pastoral leadership models."

Perhaps the Almighty had revealed to some local visionary that these activities were a part of His divine plan for Toowoomba, although visualising a God who dreamt about new "pastoral leadership models" for an outback Queensland diocese does test the imagination somewhat.

Expressions like "collaborative and participative," "enables and empowers," and "inclusiveness," provided a politically correct flavour, as did such recommendations as, "The sharing of stories of those who have chosen to resist economic pressure to conform", "All Diocesan organisations ensuring gender balance in membership where appropriate", "Indigenous Studies and Perspectives now incorporated into both curriculum and school practice", "Inclusive language in all Diocesan documents, dealings and Liturgy" and "Involvement in [Aboriginal] Reconciliation activities by all local faith communities."

The credibility of *Creating Our Future* was reflected in its recommendation of Michael Morwood's book, *Tomorrow's Church*. A theological analysis of this book in 1998 revealed so many flaws that Archbishop Pell curtailed its use in the Melbourne Archdiocese.

Under the heading of "Developing and Updating Adult Faith Education and Spirituality" the following books were also recommended: *Eucharist: Participating in Mystery* by Fr Frank Andersen MSC (a former adult education colleague of Michael Morwood with similar views), *Journeys by Heart: a Christology of Erotic Power* by the American feminist theologian, Rita Brock, *In Search of Belief* by Sr Joan Chittister OSB (an American doctrinal dissenter and radical feminist) and *The Meaning of the Sacraments* by Monika Hellwig (a feminist US academic, whose writings have conflicted with Church teachings.

Another section of *Creating Our Future* was titled "Promoting and Celebrating Life-giving Liturgy" and included among its recommended references the discredited American document, *Environment and Art in Catholic Worship*, which was then in process of being replaced by the American bishops. This document had received no approval from the US bishops' conference at the time it was published by a committee in 1978, yet it has long been used by the Church's architectural experts in a number of countries as justification for vandalising beautiful cathedral and church interiors or as a guide for designing barren, soulless barn-like new church structures.

Some "Action Paths" listed for "Promoting and Celebrating Life-giving Liturgy" included, "Encouraging the use of creative penitential services in parishes", "Promoting liturgy that is culturally, spiritually, and gender inclusive", "Liturgical experiences that are more relevant", "Liturgical experiences that are nurturing" and "Liturgical experiences that create more consciousness for life in the world."

If these and similar attempts to add relevance and sparkle to the liturgy have somehow failed to entice the Church's lost sheep back to the pews, at least they keep a few liturgists off the dole.

Finally, the program's incessant use of the expression "dream" (or "dreaming") underlined its pervasive unreality, given the ongoing crisis of faith and the readily available resources for addressing it, such as the *Catechism of the Catholic Church*.

The story was similar throughout much of Queensland over this period, as it was in other states' similarly run dioceses. The following case study is not untypical.

Rockhampton

The Queensland Diocese of Rockhampton has been moving in a "spirit of Vatican II" direction since the Council due to a series of liberal bishops. With the appointment of Bishop Brian Heenan to succeed Bishop Bernard Wallace in 1990, the momentum was maintained.

An early example of this "newchurch" approach materialised with the circulation of a "Nomination Form" throughout the diocese prior to the absence of all parish priests for a 12-day "in-service" at the Iwasaki Resort at Yeppoon to begin on 6 September 1993.[8]

The Nomination Form invited Catholics to elect their own "presiders" at prayer services. "I would like", it read, "to nominate the following people to lead our community in parish prayer on the weekend of 11-12 September during the priests' in-service."

Bishop Heenan explained his move in an Easter Message. "Easter," he said, "is a time of new life and an invitation to build new visions for the future. I think especially of our Diocese and I have asked our priests to come away together for an extended time of renewal this year. Their numbers are reducing, the Church is passing through unprecedented change and our expectation of priests is different ... I ask each of you to send them with a blessing and to accept a weekend without Masses. As a bishop I am able to dispense you from the Sunday obligation for a good reason and I do so for the benefit of our priests and our diocese".

Lest anyone question the Bishop's "good reason", the late Dr Peter Young, then Rockhampton's Director of Catholic Adult Education and Editor of the diocesan monthly, declared in his regular column in *The Review*, "If the bishop, after due deliberation, prayer and consultation, requires the withdrawal of the pastors from their parishes for a particular (in the bishop's estimation) serious reason, it ill-behoves us to challenge such a movement of the Holy Spirit."[9]

Dr Young's stern reminder was necessary as some Rockhampton Catholics had dared question the wisdom of a Mass-less weekend.

Preparations for the "in-service" continued week by week. Mass bulletins for 25 July 1993 advised parishioners that "Bishop Brian has dispensed us from our Sunday obligation, but we are not dispensed from our Sunday observance. Therefore, on this weekend we will gather for Parish Prayer in our churches. Members of our parish community will preside at this prayer". Notice was given that over the following weekend, people would be given opportunity to nominate three people "as suitable presiders."

The following weekend Mass bulletins reported, "The Diocesan Liturgical Commission has commenced its program which prepares those who will be responsible for the Parish Prayer and other pastoral care in the regions of the diocese during the priests' absence in September."

The Commission was to conduct a workshop at the Cathedral College Hall on 14 August, titled "When There is No Priest", which it said would "help prepare lay people for leadership roles in liturgies and/or ministry to the sick."

At Masses prior to this "in-service", parishioners were required to proclaim their loyal support for the priest-less and Mass-less weekend. The Mass bulletins dictated words for recitation: "As members of this parish community, we fully support you, Father, as you join your fellow priests for a time of renewal, sharing of ideas, companionship and spiritual growth. We are happy to accept our lay presiders as they continue the work of sharing the gospel message."

The preparation for a priestless Rockhampton was none too soon. Shortly after the Yeppoon gathering, two Rockhampton priests (including the Administrator of the Cathedral) left the priesthood while another took unspecified leave of absence for 12 months. In fact, during Bishop Heenan's time, at least ten priests have left the priesthood out of an already small complement of active clergy, by 2006 down to around 30.

Dr Young, however, commented in *The Review*: "What we ALL have to learn — and very quickly — is that the Mass, 'the apex of communal celebration', is not the only way to ensure the presence of Christ in our community.

"Every time 'two or three gather in His Name' there is Christ really amongst us, we have 'eucharist.' When we gather to 'break bread' we have THE Eucharist.

"The fact that there are few priests in our parishes does NOT mean the end of the Church. In fact, it could be the Holy Spirit's way of telling the laity 'get yourselves ready, God has a new role for you to play in the life of the Church'."[10]

Church professionals

In the years following, Rockhampton seemed determined to hasten the process towards priestlessness by lowering the retiring age for priests to 70, instead of the usual 75 elsewhere. Suggestions about inviting priests from overseas or other dioceses to make up the shortfall were not taken up while priestly vocations remained practically non-existent.

But Rockhampton was not short of church professionals who were kept busy setting up conferences, meetings, discussion groups and workshops to speculate on the future of the local Church and devise more creative restructurings.

A Diocesan Conference held between 10-13 July 2000 captured something of the up-coming Olympic spirit, being titled, "Carrying the Flame: Healing, Grieving, New Beginnings." According to its all-female team of Adult Faith Co-ordinators, the conference was "a result of the successful Burning Bush Conference 1999" whose "sparks" had "inspired our Bishop to invite Diocesan Adult Faith Education and Formation" to plan another conference.[11]

These sparks ignited a veritable conflagration of workshops — 56 in all — with women religious prominent among the presenters. The following topics were quite typical and indicative of the mind-sets of those running Rockhampton:

• Bush/Creation Spirituality: "We will use our senses as we walk and sit quietly in the leafy surrounds of St Brendan's to link us with the Divine in and around us ...".

• Aboriginal Spirituality: "Taking you through a Spirituality Journey of recognising Christ speaking to you through His creation and carrying His flame to one another and one self."

• From Dirty hands to Sacred memories in your own Garden!: "Ritualising the memories of your life's journey by planning and creating your own Sacred Garden. Through reflection and focusing on the earth-directions, North, South, East and West, and connecting with one of the elements, Fire, Earth, Air and Water, the flow of life's energies will also be recognised in your plan ...".

• A Holistic experience of God through Exercise and Massage: "There will be two reflective, experiential prayer sessions. The first session, led by Sr Vera, is designed to raise awareness of the importance of preparing the body and mind to meet the challenges we face as baptised, confirmed Christians. The second, led by Sr Regina, is intended to release tensions acquired in everyday living. It opens heart, mind, body and spirit to the voice of God through massage ...".

• Equality in Relationships: "Participants in this workshop will be invited to explore a movement away from the ethics of power and control to equality in relationship by reflecting on the voices that are privileged in our society and how these voices attempt to restrain and oppress others. The workshop will offer an opportunity to discuss ways in which we can foster non-hierarchical and non-patronising relationships."

• Leading the Prayer of God's People: "This workshop explores the skills of liturgy and occasions when lay people are called to lead communal prayer. A spirituality of leading prayer will be the foundation of this workshop."

• A Child of the Universe: "In these times of rapid changes, the Universe can offer some advice in the choices we have to make. In this workshop there will be time to reflect on our lives and our relationships and to learn from the Universe so that we will be wise leaders."

The environment

Whatever else might be said of the Rockhampton Diocese, it is certainly in the forefront of environmental awareness.

A Lenten Program for 2003 was titled "Becoming Windmill People" with suggestions for "Group Ritual" including:

"Focus — a jug of water and empty glasses. Sit with the empty glasses and experience thirst.

"Focus — a bowl of earth. If you are in a group, finish the meeting by signing each other with the earth while saying the words: Repent and believe the Good News."[12]

The following year, a document published by the Rockhampton Commission for Environmental Awareness — set up by Bishop Heenan in 2003 — contained a number of suggestions on how Catholics could fine tune their green credentials.[13]

These activities were recommended for the month of February:

• Rejoice that we carry the sun in our bodies — our energy is sun energy.

• Lie on the earth and listen to its heart beat.

• Write a love letter to the Earth.

• Make your yard frog friendly.

• Play in the water.

For March, there were further ideas for the environmentally aware:

• Grieve the loss of clean water, air and fertile soil.

• Hug a tree, feel its sap rising;

• Dance in the wind.

• Feel the energy contained in the wind and sun.

• Reflect on the feminine within you — we all carry the feminine within us.

• Clean up Mother Earth's lungs.

• Be conscious of the greenhouse gases you are generating and your consumption of fossil fuels.

In 2005, a "River of Life" conference was held in Rockhampton. It was another initiative of the Diocesan Commission for Environmental Awareness.[14]

At the opening ritual, conference-goers were invited to bring water from their local parishes to add to the central symbol. The guest speakers contributed water from Kiama and several parts of Brisbane.

Thirty-three people attended, with addresses from the three "facilitators", Dermot Dorgan, a social activist and musician from Brisbane, Coralie Kingston, a former coordinator with a Church social action office, and Col Brown from Catholic Earthcare Australia.

Liturgy

Given such preoccupations, Rockhampton may well have viewed the Vatican's efforts to regulate the liturgy as distant irritants.

At a Council of Priests' meeting, Bishop Heenan reassured his shrinking band of clergy that there was very little in the 2005 Vatican Instruction *Redemptionis Sacramentum* on matters to be avoided in the Eucharist that affected "the way we celebrate Mass in Australia."

He said he was "not aware that any of the abuses highlighted in the document are being practised in the Diocese, not taking away [the] rights of special circumstances which might vary in the liturgy."

There were times, he said, "when there may be some variance from normal procedures" but he had "a great deal of trust in each priest" and respected "that styles are not all the same."[15]

During the Year of the Eucharist in 2005 Bishop Heenan presented a somewhat unusual reflection at an in-service meeting for Catholic teachers and catechists on 27 February and later at the Holy Thursday Mass of the Lord's Supper.[16]

The reflection originated from the homosexual Metropolitan Community Church of San Francisco, which described itself on its website (www.mccsf.org) as "A home for queer spirituality" and went on to declare: "We primarily serve the lesbian, gay, bisexual and transgender community".

Titled "The Eucharist", the writing in question was the work of R. Voigt, a regular contributor to the gay website. In part, it read:

"She was cute, nice build, a little too much paint,
wobbly on her feet as she slid from her barstool, and on the make.
"No thanks, not tonight." — and I gave her EUCHARIST.
"Downtown is nice,
lights change from red to green, and back again,
flashing blues, pinks and oranges:
I gulped them in,
said, 'Thank you, Father,' — and made them EUCHARIST.
"I laughed at myself, and told myself,
'You, with all your sin, and all your selfishness,

I forgive you, I accept you, I love you.'

"It's nice, and so necessary, to give yourself EUCHARIST."

The expression "Be Eucharist to one another" has already been catching on in some progressive Church circles. In Rockhampton, a four week series (concluding on 5 July 2005) organised by Adult Faith Education and Formation, and titled "Rediscovering the Eucharist", exhorted participants to "Be Eucharist for Others".[17]

The "spirit of Vatican II" continues to be alive and well in Rockhampton as it is in other similiarly "renewed" Australian dioceses.

In contrast, during the 1990s the Wagga Wagga Diocese in New South Wales under Bishop William Brennan's leadership set its sights on building up the number of priests. The result has been that this diocese now has the best ratio in Australia of active priests per Catholic population and the youngest average age for its clergy (see Chapter 10).

Great Barrier Reef

Meanwhile, if the state of the Church in their own diocesan backyards was close to terminal, Queensland's seven bishops nevertheless found the time in 2004 to focus their expertise on *A Pastoral Letter on the Great Barrier Reef* titled "Let the Many Coastlands Be Glad!"

At the launch of the glossy 26-page pastoral letter in Townsville, Bishop John Bathersby of Brisbane declared, "We believe anything that harms the reef is sinful".[18]

Bishop Heenan told *The Morning Bulletin* (Rockhampton), "Everyone has a moral responsibility to look after the reef if we want to keep this wondrous treasure". He added, "We are supporting the green zones to protect and preserve our reef for our children and our children's children".[19]

In a leaflet promoting the pastoral letter, the various "harmful human activities" compromising "the health of the reef" were listed: "emission of greenhouse gases, overfishing, poorly planned development, some tourist recreational activities and nutrient and toxic chemical run off from the coastal mainland".

The pastoral letter, however, lost credibility in referring to alleged overfishing. In fact the present fishing take from the Great Barrier Reef is negligible and there are sustainable fishing practices already in place. Any further restrictions on fishing there will mean Australia will import more and more fish from the already overfished reefs elsewhere in the Pacific region where there is no environmental management in place.

Ironically, the huge expansion of the green zones which the Queensland Bishops endorse may lead to overfishing as the best fishing grounds are closed to fishermen, who will then be forced to exploit the limited areas left, invariably causing the depletion of fish stocks.[20]

Despite its faulty research, the pastoral letter was full of spiritual good intentions, invoking John Paul II's call to an "ecological conversion", and including its own prayer to that effect:

"*God of the sun and moon*
Of the mountains, deserts and plains
God of the mighty oceans, of rivers, lakes and streams
God of all creatures that live in the seas and fly in the air
Of every living thing that grows and moves on this sacred Earth
...".[21]

Bishops Brian Heenan (Rockhampton), Michael Putney (Townsville) and Archbishop John Bathersby (Brisbane) launching the Queensland Bishops' Pastoral Letter on the Great Barrier Reef (2004)
Photograph © Courier Mail *(Brisbane)*

Religious Orders: greener pastures

Following the Second Vatican Council, it was the larger religious orders, particularly those involved in Catholic education, that were most quickly swept along by the "spirit of Vatican II". As their numbers in schools dwindled, vocations disappeared and average age rose (today close on 70), some members of these orders sought the greener pastures of radical feminism, environmentalism, New Age neo-paganism or combinations of these.

In 2001, a controversy erupted in Brisbane over a so-called "Womenspace" which operated from a building owned by the Presentation Sisters and involved members of the Mercy Sisters order.

Fr Paul Stenhouse MSC, editor of the national monthly religious journal *Annals*, and a well-known scholar, commented at the time, "Adding to the incongruity of associating Catholic personnel with blatantly pantheistic and 'green' feminist 'rituals' we discover that the 'mystery of Womenspace' has been made possible by the Presentation Sisters who bought the property, and the Mercy Sisters, who pay the salary of Anne McLay, the chairwoman.

"Since the '60s, many of the schools that religious orders once ran in the name of Catholicism vied with one another in becoming pluralistic, ecumenical and post-Vatican II in every way. Their summons to a fresher and greener future without 'absolutist theology' or 'authoritarian' male clergy forms the melody line we hear being sung by feminist nuns."[22]

In one of many feature articles published on the subject in Brisbane's daily newspaper, *The Courier-Mail*, the writer remarked, "Bad enough, some think, that a Catholic nun is conducting ceremonies that draw on Celtic rituals and traditions that pre-date St Patrick's conversion of pagan Ireland or that the centre provides material advertising lesbian and witchcraft activities.

"More damning has been this week's revelation that [the pro-abortion] Children by Choice, a group totally at odds with Catholic beliefs, held its annual general meeting there, on Church property".[23]

Archbishop Bathersby initially seemed reluctant to tackle the controversy ("Religious sisters and brothers do make mistakes, as we all do in trying to follow Christ"), pointing the finger instead at those he called "true believers" who had reported on illicit general absolutions in his archdiocese and in other Queensland dioceses. However, under considerable pressure with the continuing media coverage of the scandal, he eventually set in motion an investigation of sorts.[24]

Five years on, Womenspace continues to use the Presentation Order's property. A Mercy nun, Sr Anne McLay, is secretary and runs a "Celtic Spirituality" program which is described as follows on the Womenspace website:[25]

"The ancient Celts saw all of life as holy. Through their many goddess images of the divine, the Celts particularly honoured the feminine. They revered the sacred as revealed in the land and worshipped in the woods and by the waters. Celtic spirituality is having a renewal today as we are facing the disastrous results of having devalued the feminine and having severed our sense of oneness with the land and its non-human inhabitants."

In 2006, a Womenspace publication indicated the kind of focus some of today's religious favour. "From February to April", it said, "we re-membered the power of wild women, especially the wild women within ourselves. In particular, we expressed the power at our Conversation Circle; gave it some form within the paintings and other contributions to the Installation; celebrated the triple spiral of virgin, mother, crone with Glenys Livingstone; entered with Persephone into the darkness of the Underworld at the Autumn Equinox; honoured all women, especially indigenous women, at our International Women's Day Breakfast; kicked up our heels on High Spirited Day; met Lilith, the goddess of the Dark Moon with Jenni Monks; and wondered if we were really wicked witches or what ... with a video of the Burning Times".[26]

A Social Action Office, based in Brisbane, was founded in 1992 by the Conference of Leaders of Religious Institutes, Queensland, "to undertake and cultivate social action ministry". The Office serves a statewide network of Catholic Religious Congregations in Queensland and also works closely with Religious Congregations across Australia. Its links page includes a list of "links to relevant websites". Under the category "spirituality", its links include Womenspace (Brisbane).[27]

The Sisters of Mercy now have an eco-centre north of Brisbane, called Earth Link (Connecting People and Earth). Its "Spirituality Statement" has a pantheistic flavour: "In our times, there are ongoing shifts in our knowledge about the unfolding story of the universe, the nature of matter, the interconnectedness of the web of life, the important ancient Earth traditions ... Many people are seeking to make meaning of their knowledge of these changes, to their own connections with nature and the cosmos, and to name their experience of the Sacred".[28]

Earth Link further invites those interested to "listen to the wisdom of Earth", "explore your relationship with the Earth community", "acknowledge the Sacred within the whole web of life", "celebrate with awe and wonder all that this inspires" and "live in the right relationship that this calls forth".

A similar body, Eco-Justice, is described as "the work of the [Christian] Brothers and the wider Edmund Rice Network". Information from the website describes how the Christian Brothers in 2002 "took a radical new step in their self-understanding and their mission. They began to focus on what their hearts were telling them". This led to "a passion for social justice" recognising "that Edmund's charism included a Spirit-inspired move to change the very structures of his society".

However, we are told, "the Spirit led them further" as "they heard the yearning of the Earth itself for healing and re-generation". The Brothers, consequently, "committed themselves to 'radical relationships of equality with all of God's creation'."[29]

In Melbourne, another entity, titled EarthSong, has surfaced in recent years. Its initial co-sponsors were the Brigidine Sisters, Christian Brothers, FCJ Sisters, Loreto Sisters, Presentation Sisters and Mercy Sisters, with several other unnamed orders providing funds for the project.

The EarthSong website provides abundant information on its activities, resources and "spirituality", with references to a "new cosmology", "ways of honouring the sacredness of all creation" and rituals to celebrate nature — none of them suggesting any connection at all with the Judeo-Christian tradition, let alone Catholicism.[30]

According to the "Vision Statement" of the "Co-sponsoring Congregations", EarthSong "had its genesis in a conversation between members of several religious orders in Melbourne in early 2003". Each of these "found a resonance between the vision of 'celebrating the sacred in all of creation' and their Order's vision, inspirational documents and directional statements."

During 2006, sessions on "Exploring the New Cosmology" were scheduled at several Victorian Catholic venues. Among the offerings was "Celebrating Cosmogenesis: The Triple Spiral in the Seasonal Wheel ... based on the content of the aforementioned Glenys Livingstone's recent publication *PaGaian Cosmology*, which explores an eco-spirituality grounded in indigenous Western religious celebration of the Earth-Sun annual cycle" — Gaia being the name of an ancient Earth goddess.

Here, participants were to be "involved in an experiential workshop developing ritual in the context of the current season".

Among the recommended book titles on the EarthSong site are *The Sacred Earth: Writers on Nature and Spirit*, edited by Jason Gardner, *PaGaian Cosmology: Re-inventing Earth-based Goddess Religion* by Glenys Livingstone, *The Sacred Balance: Rediscovering Our Place in Nature* by David Suzuki with Amanda McConnell and *The Dream of the Earth* by Thomas Berry.

Other recommended resources include: *Earth Prayers from around the World: 365 Prayers, Poems and Invocations for Honouring The Earth*, edited by Elizabeth Roberts and Elias Amidon, *The Star In My Heart: Experiencing Sophia, Inner Wisdom* by Joyce Rupp, *Prayers for a Planetary Pilgrim: A Personal Manual for Prayer and Ritual* by Edward Hays, *Sparks of The Cosmos: Rituals for Seasonal Use* by Margaret Abbott RSM, *Sparks of Life: Rituals for Children* by Margaret Abbott RSM and Jennifer Callanan, and *Celebrating The Great Mother: A Handbook of Earth-Honoring Activities for Parents and Children* by Cait Johnson and Maura D. Shaw.

These book and resource titles speak for themselves.

The cult of nature and even pre-Christian paganism appear to be gradually subsuming some of Australia's dying religious communities.

Endnotes

1. Quoted from original diocesan documents in *AD2000*, October 1989, pp. 12-13.
2. Ibid.
3. "The Catholic Church in Adelaide: road to renewal or decline?", *AD2000*, February 1997, p. 6.
4. "Brisbane Archdiocese booklets: how to make parishes 'zoom along'," *AD2000*,

April 1997, p. 5.
5. *The Catholic Leader* (Brisbane), 2 March 1997.
6. *AD2000*, October 2000, p. 4.
7. *Creating Our Future*, Diocese of Toowoomba, 2000, cited in *AD2000*, November 2000, pp. 6-7.
8. *The Sunday Mail* (Rockhampton), 23 May 1993, p. 23; *AD2000*, November 1993, p. 10.
9. *The Review* (Rockhampton Diocese), May 1993.
10. Ibid.
11. Quoted in *AD2000*, August 2000, p. 8.
12. Lenten Program for the Diocese of Rockhampton, "Becoming Windmill People", Life in Drought, Week One.
13. Quoted in A*D2000*, April 2004, p. 5.
14. *AD2000*, December 2005-January 2006, p.5.
15. Minutes of the Diocese of Rockhampton Council of Priests' Meeting, 3 June 2004.
16. MCC San Francisco: A Home for Queer Spirituality, "The Eucharist", R. Voigt, 22 December 2004. Bishop Heenan's use of this as a reflection was confirmed by people who attended the in-service and Mass.
17. Adult Faith & Formation, Diocese of Rockhampton, "Rediscovering the Eucharist", 24 May-5 July 2005.
18. *Townsville Bulletin*, 7 August 2004.
19. *The Morning Bulletin* (Rockhampton), 12 August 2004.
20. "Catholic Earthcare Australia adopts discredited Green agenda", Pat Byrne, *AD2000*, December 2004-January 2005, p. 6.
21. *A Pastoral Letter on the Great Barrier Reef*, "Let the Many Coastlands Be Glad!", Catholic Bishops of Queensland, 2004.
22. *The Courier-Mail,* 17 November 2001, p. 32.
23. Ibid.
24. Ibid.
25. www.womenspace.org.au/
26. *Womenspace News*, Edition 2, May-August 2006, p. 1.
27. www.sao.clriq.org.au/about.html; www.sao.clriq.org.au/links.html
28. Earth Link: Connecting People and Earth, 11 June 2006, http://earth-link.org.au/spirituality.html
29. www.ecojustice.edmundclt.org/background/background.html
30. www.earthsong.org.au/programs/index.html

Chapter Three

"Shadows" in the Liturgy

In 2003, in his last encyclical *Ecclesia de Eucharistia*, Pope John Paul II referred to "shadows" in the liturgy brought about by a defective implementation of the Second Vatican Council's liturgical reforms which had led to numerous abuses.

The Vatican II Constitution on the Sacred Liturgy, *Sacrosanctum Concilium,* provided the framework for subsequent changes to the Church's Latin Rite liturgy. However, during the 40 years since the document was approved by the world's bishops at the Council, many of its recommendations have been distorted or disregarded.

The bottom line requirement was spelt out clearly (22, 3): "Therefore no other person, not even a priest, may add, remove, or change anything in the liturgy on his own authority".

This is because the liturgy is not the personal property of individual priests, congregations or liturgists. It belongs to the universal Church.

Other requirements of the Vatican II liturgy document might come as a surprise to many of today's Catholics, for example, the retention of Latin in the Mass (36, 1) while permitting some use of the vernacular, and "pride of place" to be given to Gregorian chant (116).

With the use of vernacular, problems have arisen since the first officially approved English translation of the Missal was launched in the 1970s. In hindsight, the language is now seen to lack the sacred quality needed for worship of God, while gross inaccuracies abound, crying out for correction. These deficiencies are being currently addressed with translation guidelines provided by *Liturgiam Authenticam*, a document issued at the direction of Pope John Paul II.

A further problem area, the numerous abuses in the liturgy, involving such practices as non-Scriptural readings, changed wordings to prayers, or omissions of parts of the Mass, prompted a further document, *Redemptionis Sacramentum*, also published at John Paul II's direction as a follow-up to his encyclical *Ecclesia de Eucharistia*.

These, and other authoritative Church documents provide the proper reference points for what is or is not permitted in Catholic worship. Unfortunately, they continue to be disregarded by those who should know better, while most people in the pews remain in blissful ignorance of their existence, let alone their contents.

This means that liturgy today remains the Church's most visible problem area, for it is where Catholics encounter their faith most directly and often. Their perception of what this faith means is largely governed by the state of the liturgy and how the priest celebrates it in their parish.

As Fr Peter Williams, Director of the Liturgy Commission of the Diocese of Parramatta and Executive Officer of the National Liturgical Commission, pointed out, "Given that the liturgy is for most Catholic people their principal exposure to the public life of the Church, and for many their only opportunity to be exposed to any formation, then the body of prayers that make up the Church's liturgy must be authentic and faithful in expressing the deposit of faith and the Latin tradition of the Church".[1]

In fact, many of the changes in the liturgy now accepted as "normal" were not called for by the Second Vatican Council but were often the work of liturgists with their own agenda implementing "the spirit of Vatican II". Moreover, the general consensus today, with the advantage of hindsight, is that the process of liturgical renewal was very poorly handled and caused much pastoral damage.

Monsignor Peter J. Elliott, Episcopal Vicar for Religious Education in the Melbourne Archdiocese, who has written extensively on liturgy, offered the following explanation for this situation.[2]

"Basically", he said, "the work of the liturgical movement and Pius XII in *Mediator Dei* on the meaning and spirit of the liturgy was not properly assimilated before the Council.

"The opening doctrinal section of *Sacrosanctum Concilium* is brief, because it presupposes *Mediator Dei*. Then, after the Council, the 'changes' were introduced in an authoritarian way, hastily, often without respect for popular piety and what people valued. Extremists and cranks soon moved in, experimenting, innovating and pushing people around. They moved many altars but not so many hearts.

"I also believe that some changes to the Mass went beyond what the Council Fathers envisaged in *Sacrosanctum Concilium*, and this is the very area where we still encounter problems. We also need to remember that the late 1960s and 1970s was an era of cultural modernism, marked by overconfidence, radical chic and bad taste."

In 2003, Cardinal Francis George of Chicago reviewed the changes since the Council observing that "numerous and rapid changes in ritual forms can produce estrangement and anomie — an experience reported by many of the faithful in the post-conciliar years".[3]

Officially approved innovations like the widespread use of lay people to distribute Holy Communion, receiving Communion on the hand, and standing instead of kneeling to receive were not required by the Council and although individually capable of justification, in combination they could erode Eucharistic faith.

Likewise, the removal in many churches of altar rails, pulpits, kneelers, confessionals, high altars and assorted religious art works — none of them specifically called for by Vatican II — made the environment for worship appear increasingly sterile and unstable, fuelling the belief that the Church had fundamentally changed.

The inferior, supermarket English Mass translation used since the early 1970s added to the trend, while making it easier for priests so inclined to introduce their own variations in wordings, including so-called inclusive language.

Msgr Elliott, comments, "I hope that the Vox Clara committee [set up by John Paul II to supervise a new Missal translation] will put one problem behind us — the poor English translations. We have suffered 30 years of banal and inaccurate texts. That scandal is on a par with the mistranslated vernacular Bibles that spread errors at the time of the Reformation."[4]

Another common occurrence was alluded to by Cardinal Francis

Arinze, Prefect of the Congregation for the Divine Liturgy and the Discipline of the Sacraments, who said recently, "If he [the priest] is not very disciplined he will soon become a performer. He may not realise it, but he will be projecting himself rather than projecting Christ. Indeed it is very demanding, the altar facing the people."[5]

The Liturgy, he stressed, "is not the property of one individual, therefore an individual does not tinker with it, but makes the effort to celebrate it as Holy Mother Church wants. When that happens, the people are happy, they feel nourished. Their faith grows, their faith is strengthened. They go home happy and [are] willing to come back next Sunday".

Over the past 30 years this has not been happening for a large proportion of Australian Catholics.

Priests educated in the seminaries since the late 1960s — meaning most of today's active priests — were generally formed liturgically in a creative, communitarian direction and while some of the declining number of Mass-attending Catholics find this style to their liking, having long become accustomed to it as normal, others disenchanted at the absence of any sense of the sacred have gravitated to Latin Masses or given up altogether.

The worst of the post-Vatican II excesses may be over, but to judge from personal observations and feedback from Catholics in different dioceses, it seems abuses are still occurring to a greater or lesser extent.

This perception is shared by Msgr Elliott. "There has been some stabilisation," he noted, "and the revised Roman Missal and General Instruction should help, but there are still widespread problems — sloppy ceremonial, verbosity, vulgar music, disobedience and sheer ignorance."[6]

The worst instances of these tend to be found at school and college Masses, weddings, funerals, First Communions or on major commemorative occasions where the creative impulses of those involved tend to override the Church's liturgical requirements.

The following examples illustrate these observations.

Misguided creativity

Among the more recent examples of misguided creativity was an end of year Mass at Mt Alvernia College, Brisbane, titled "Look to the Stars — Follow Our Dreams". The Mass booklet's contents seemed guided more by New Age ideas and political correctness than the Catholic Church's liturgical rubrics.[7]

The Entrance Song consisted of "Under Southern Skies," as sung by Nikki Webster at the 2000 Sydney Olympics opening ceremony, while at the Penitential Rite, the celebrant said, "O God, you who are Mother and Father to us all". At the time when the Nicene Creed would normally be recited, all were invited to remain seated and "pray this statement of beliefs". The credal concoction read in part:

"I believe in God who created man and woman in God's image who created the world and gave both sexes the care of the earth. I believe in Jesus child of God chosen of God born of the woman Mary, who listened to women and liked them, who stayed in their homes, who discussed the kingdom with them, who was followed and financed by women and disciples.

"I believe in Jesus who received anointing from a woman at Simon's house, who rebuked the male guests who scorned her. I believe in Jesus who spoke of himself as a mother hen who would gather her chicks under her wing".

Then followed what was described as an "adapted" Lord's Prayer:

"God, our provider and creator, you are bigger than our little world. You call us beyond our everyday limits to higher things. Your presence in our lives gives us a sense of wonder and awe. We long for the dream of creating a new and better earth. May we live and act in harmony with your will in helping to create a happier world. We ask you, God, for what we need each day — food, drink, love, challenge, a sense of community — may all of us experience the fulfilment of these needs. We ask for reconciliation with you, our God, and with others. We ask you, God, to shelter and care for us always".

During the Sign of Peace, a poem, titled "You are Special", was read out, including references to "hopes and dreams" and "beams" from shooting stars. The Reflection after Communion continued the New Age flavour with a song titled "Just One Star":

"*Shining sun of a far off moon,*
Hear my heart and answer soon,
Glimmer bright so far away,
Awake the dawn and light a bright new day ...".

The Recessional Song was "Dare to Dream" as performed by John Farnham and Olivia Newton-John at the Sydney Olympics.

At a Commissioning Ceremony for new student representative councillors for St Saviour's College, a girls' boarding school in Toowoomba, Queensland, in 2002, the Mass booklet was labelled "Celebrating Catherine McAuley — The Dance of Woman".[8]

The liturgy consisted of an opening "Sprinkling Rite" performed by two students and a "Story Telling" segment involving three students. The Gospel Acclamation read: "You are a light for the whole world, Woman, your light must shine".

After the Gospel was read by one of the students, there was "A Conversation with Mrs Carmel Seng". During the "Prayers of the Community", the response was "We hear the dance of the heavenly Woman".

A "Final Blessing" was given by a Mrs Christine Ryan.

This is reminiscent of one south-east Queensland parish church which was "blessed" by the parishioners.

During 2000, a "Dzintari Earth Care Outdoor Mass" was celebrated in a parish of the Adelaide Archdiocese. The booklet acknowledged help from the Diocesan Earth Team, Raywood Nursery, Normanville Liturgy Group and St Luke's Folk Group.[9]

The Opening Hymn commenced with the immortal words,

"*Hear the humpback singing from the sea,*
With the message for you and me:
The dolphins and the coral reef,
The fishes in the ocean deep,
They won't survive
Unless we hear their plea ...".

The Nicene Creed was replaced, this time by an "Australian Prayer", which included the words "We believe in Australians, in their courage and spirit of adventure, in their perseverance and hard work, in their ordinariness and at homeness, in their black Aboriginal beauty, in their migrant struggles, in their search for identity ...".

A final illustration is provided by an "Aboriginal & Torres Strait Islanders Mass for the Year of the Indigenous People" that was celebrated at St Joseph's Cathedral, Rockhampton.[10]

The Introductory Rites involved the Bishop and priests going to the altar "preceded by the Woorabinda Aboriginal dancers". There, according to the Mass booklet, "The Dance and Smoke Ceremony take the place of the penitential rite".

At the Offertory, "Wandjina" was played, while "Soil — a symbol of the sacred places is brought forward" along with Torres-Strait emblems. During the Recessional, "Traditional Torres Strait Islander sacred music" was played.

These are just a few examples of how the Church's official form of worship can easily be hijacked, in the process undermining the faith handed down from the Apostles. To address this crisis, all involved in liturgy planning, including members of diocesan and parish liturgy bodies and teachers in Catholic schools and colleges, need a solid re-education — via in-services — on the contents of the recently revised *General Instruction of the Roman Missal* and *Redemptoris Sacramentum*. The latter, as indicated earlier (see page 40), itemises practices to be eliminated from concocted liturgies so that the Universal Church can once more pray what she believes.

Allowing liturgies to be taken over by assorted causes and big occasions, however significant, trivialises the Mass and distracts attention from what it is about. The ancient and revered aphorism, *Lex orandi, lex credendi*, loosely translated, means, as people pray, so do they believe.

Different agenda

It is now over 25 years since John Paul II issued *Dominicae Cenae* and authorised *Inaestimabile Donum*, documents which set out clearly what is required in liturgical celebrations. Yet some members of Australia's liturgical establishment still pursue their own agenda, viewing any directives from the Holy See with undisguised hostility. It is no wonder so little improvement — where it is most needed — is evident at the grass roots.

Brisbane, in particular, has long regarded itself as the most liturgically progressive diocese in Australia, with its liturgists and celebrants seemingly granted open slather.

The revamped interior of St Stephen's Cathedral (as of 1990) — with hidden tabernacle, monstrous statue of a Christ figure floating over the altar table, and Aboriginal dreamtime space near the entrance — is a potent symbol of Queensland's approach to worship.

Fr Tom Elich, former Director of the National Liturgical Commission, Director of Brisbane's Liturgical Commission, editor of *Liturgy News*, the Commission's Quarterly Bulletin, and a member of ICEL's Advisory Committee from 1990 to 1997, has long been outspoken — his views being fairly typical of some members of Australia's liturgical establishment, many of whom contribute to *Liturgy News*.

Fr Elich expressed public "dismay" when the Vatican refused permission for an inclusive language New Revised Standard Version lectionary for Masses. He told Brisbane's archdiocesan weekly that "the implications of the [Vatican] ban are very serious for Catholic biblical scholarship, for ecumenical relations between Churches, as well as for the production of suitable liturgical books".[11]

When the new *General Instruction on the Roman Missal* was published in 2000, he commented, "The impression is unavoidable, however, that the Holy See is trying to accommodate liturgical lobby groups. I regret this because I believe that lobby groups are unhelpful, particularly in the Church". The General Instruction, he said, seemed "to presume irregularities in practice", contained "cautions and detailed regulations" and "excessive spelling-out" of instructions, and had "a defensive tone".[12]

In 2001, Fr Elich was displeased with the Vatican Instruction, *Liturgiam Authenticam*, which had John Paul II's endorsement. "I believe", he said, "the document itself is a betrayal on two levels: firstly with respect to the language we will use to worship God in our liturgy, and secondly with respect to the bishops' responsibility for preparing and approving liturgical books in the vernacular".

He questioned the Instruction's emphasis on words and expressions which "differ from usual and everyday speech" in order to better convey "heavenly realities" and expressed concern that politically correct "inclusive language is dismissed as an inauthentic development".

He concluded, "If we use in liturgy language which reflects an unjust world view or the sinful structures of a culture, then the liturgy will be compromised".[13]

Fr Elich was particularly piqued at the release of *Redemptionis Sacramentum*. It consolidated, he said, "a return to a negative, legalistic and rubrical approach to the worthy celebration of the Church's liturgy", adding that he found Benedict XVI's "quite negative assessment of the liturgical reform of the last forty years" to be "troubling". [14]

During 2005, Fr Elich spoke out against certain "lobby groups" which had led the Synod on the Eucharist to recommend an "exaggerated" focus on "the place of adoration and eucharistic devotions in the guise of promoting greater reverence towards the blessed Sacrament". He was also displeased at the "big push from those who seek to reverse the Church's guidelines on the placement of the tabernacle in a worthy chapel of its own, returning it to a central place in the sanctuary".[15]

He neglected to specify which "guidelines" he had in mind simply because there are no guidelines of any official standing necessitating the removal of tabernacles from a central position on sanctuaries.

In a 2006 editorial, Fr Elich rejected the very idea of "the reform of the reform, that is, the desire to have another run at the liturgical reform and produce a different (and more conservative) result". Cardinal Ratzinger, now Benedict XVI, was a strong advocate of this approach in his writings on liturgy.

For Fr Elich, this contradicted the "spirit of Vatican II". "The presumption," he said, "is that the reform of the liturgy undertaken by the Second Vatican Council has gone off the rails and itself is in need of a reform. To my way of thinking this betrays a lack of trust in the presence and action of the Holy Spirit in the Council and an indictment of the direction in which the Holy Spirit has led the Church these last few decades".[16]

Cardinal Francis George of Chicago, himself a noted liturgist, thought differently. Liturgical renewal after the Council, he believed, had shown in hindsight a "kind of naive innocence", with inadequate "thought being given to what happens in any community when its symbol system is disrupted".[17]

Sacraments

Typical of the products of Brisbane's Liturgical Commission under Fr Elich's direction was the publication, *Sacraments of Confirmation and Eucharist* [18] which in Brisbane are celebrated together early in primary school.

Its watch-words are "meal" and "community" but not "sacrifice" and "real presence". The style is '70s "experiential", e.g., "Make rainbow place mats to use at a special family meal", or "Try doing things with your hands tied behind your back".

A "Parent Reflection" states, "When the Christian community meets to celebrate the eucharist, Jesus is present. We recognise his presence in the gathering of the baptised, in the leadership of the priest, in the proclamation of the Scriptures, and in the consecrated bread and wine we share. Jesus said, 'Do this in memory of me.' In the eucharist we remember Jesus' self-giving love".[19]

While Vatican II noted the senses in which Christ could be present, it underlined that he is present "especially in the eucharistic species". This view was repeatedly affirmed by John Paul II.[20]

However, the Brisbane booklet asserts, "The first symbol in the eucharist is the Church assembled. So the sacramental signs are not just bread and wine, but the ritual of taking, breaking, sharing and eating the bread, taking, pouring out, sharing and drinking the wine. The meal is an essential aspect of eucharist".[21]

This appears to downplay the real presence of Jesus Christ, under the appearance of bread and wine, following the consecration. It also bypasses the essential sacrificial character of the Mass, a point often emphasised by John Paul II during his pontificate.

Similar approaches — with the tendency to over-stress community at the expense of sacrificial worship — have continued to be promoted in other Australian dioceses, impacting particularly on school and parish sacramental programs.

St Mary's Church, South Brisbane, the church that gave out chocolate frogs during a Mass for children, could fill out this entire chapter from its communal "Consecration" to its former use of "creator, liberator and sustainer" instead of "Father, Son and Holy Spirit" — a practice stopped by Archbishop Bathersby in 2004.

Extraordinary ministers

The exalted role of the laity since Vatican II, mistakenly interpreted as requiring more lay people on sanctuaries rather than providing a Christian leaven in the secular world, has seen the needless proliferation of so-called "special ministers of the Eucharist". Their correct title, as *Redemptionis Sacramentum* makes clear, is "Extraordinary Ministers of Holy Communion", and as the word "extraordinary" suggests, their use should be the exception rather than the rule.

The Church allows their use for the distribution of Communion when there is a likelihood of Mass being unduly prolonged due to an especially large congregation, the infirmity of the celebrant, or the absence of assistant priests.

This is not the case at many of today's Masses, particularly with attendances in decline, but the use of "special ministers" as they continue to be called, has become a settled routine.

In many parishes, casually dressed lay people move about the sanctuary, sometimes in a laid-back manner, even removing ciboriums from the tabernacle. The effect of this week after week is to diminish a sense of the sacred as well as the essential sacramental role of the priest.

The former Apostolic Pro Nuncio, Archbishop Francesco Canalini, drew attention to this phenomenon during an address to a group of religious in 2004. "I mention also," he said, "the [routine] use of 'extraordinary ministers' of Holy Communion in cases not of real need, as is the rule. These ministers sometimes distribute Holy Communion even when priests are available and remain seated. This practice as a way of manifesting an active role of lay people in the Eucharistic celebration can unfortunately direct attention more and more to the merely human and 'social' dimension".[22]

These days, with the practice now well entrenched and so many acting in good faith, most priests and bishops prefer not to insist on upholding the Church's discipline when there are too few at Mass to justify use of Extraordinary Ministers, lest they cause hurt feelings or arguments.

The farcical situation that has been allowed to become established is illustrated by the following example, which commonly occurs across Australia.

In my own parish in the Ballarat Diocese, "special ministers" had been rostered for over 20 years, helping out at weekend Masses even when relatively few were present. When Communion under both species was introduced a few years ago, the priest began distributing the hosts on his own while two "special ministers" assisted with the chalices, although only a small proportion of the congregation chose to receive from these. With the priest now distributing the hosts on his own there has been no noticeable or untoward prolongation of the Mass.

Re-education

With the vast majority of Australian Catholics no longer fulfilling their Sunday Mass obligation, and repair work long overdue, it may be too late to reverse the drift. Whatever the case, the following areas call for urgent re-education for the benefit of those attending Mass now and in the future.

• **Observing rubrics**: Priests must stick to the liturgical texts. Canon 846, §1 frrom the new *Code of Canon Law* states, "The liturgical books approved by the competent authority are to be faithfully observed in the celebration of the sacraments; therefore no one on personal authority may add, remove or change anything in them".

Where this is not being done, bishops should move promptly and decisively if there are grounds for action. One or two examples would send a message to other offenders.

• **A sense of the sacred**: Priests and bishops need to foster a greater sense of the sacred, including an attitude of reverence, a prayerful sign of the cross with holy water on entering, an unhurried genuflection and the absence of unnecessary conversation and noise before and after Mass. Socialising should be done outside the church.

• **The Mass as a sacrifice**: An appreciation of the Mass as a sacrifice needs more emphasis. As *Redemptionis Sacramentum* reminds us[23], "The constant teaching of the church on the nature of the Eucharist is that it is not only a meal, but also and preeminently a sacrifice". John Paul II underlined this in his encyclical *Ecclesia de Eucharistia*: "The sacrifice of Christ and the sacrifice of the Eucharist are one single sacrifice ... the Mass makes present the sacrifice of the Cross".[24]

• **The Real Presence**: Stronger teaching on the real presence of Jesus Christ in the Eucharist is needed. John Paul II reminded Catholics in *Ecclesia de Eucharistia*, "The sacramental re-presentation of Christ's sacrifice, crowned by the resurrection, in the Mass involves a most special presence which — in the words of Paul VI — 'is called "real" not as a way of excluding all other types of presence as if they were "not real", but because it is a presence in the fullest sense: a substantial presence whereby Christ, the God-Man, is wholly and entirely present'".[25]

Following from this is the need for priests and bishops to promote Eucharistic adoration.

• **Community over-emphasised**: The exaggerated emphasis on "community" as the central symbol of the Mass needs to be addressed, with a stronger focus on worship of God. The sign of peace has not always helped in this regard.

According to Bishop Kevin Manning of Parramatta, "The consequences of it being 'our Church' are enormous and are reflected in many of the abuses we encounter because it means we have departed from our roots. If it is merely 'our Church' then we are justified in doing away with the hierarchy, rejecting Christ's authority and being ruled by a consensus of the majority of the members of the organisation.

"In the question of liturgy we are dealing with the very core of Christian faith, so in experimenting with liturgy we need to be very, very clear that we are experimenting with the nature of the Church.

"Liturgy is not an expression of what is current and transitory, for it expresses the 'Mystery of the Holy' and enduring. Those who want liturgy devised by the community according to their own mind will finish up with a liturgy measured by its effect as a spectacle, or entertainment — this, without understanding that human beings cannot make something which manifests the holiness of God".[26]

• **Participation**: Vatican II's encouragement of greater participation at Mass has been a major source of misunderstanding. While the English translation of the Council's liturgy document called for "active" participation, the Latin word it used was not "activa" but "actuosa" — better translated as "actual". *Redemptionis Sacramentum* explains: "Active [actual] participation in the liturgy does not imply that everyone must necessarily have something to do beyond the actions and gestures".[27]

The common practice since Vatican II has been to interpret "participation" as requiring as many lay people as possible *doing* things on the sanctuary while providing as many opportunities as possible for movement and speaking by members of the congregation — even to the extent of incorporating drama and dance into the liturgy. The English word "active" seems to justify such activities, while "actual" participation is more consistent with prayerful understanding, attentiveness, quiet reflection on what is taking place during Mass and personal commitment to the mysteries of faith being celebrated.

Bishop Manning points out that the Council included silence under "active participation". This silence, he says, "helps to attain a deep personal participation and allows us to listen inwardly to the Lord's words. This becomes more difficult nowadays because of the noise which abounds in our churches.

"If the inner dimension is neglected then we will find our liturgies boring, unintelligible, and chasing the development of a kind of 'party atmosphere.' It leads to people providing their own action in place of the deep contemplative following of the Mass, which is a shared action at a much deeper level".[28]

• **Church renovations**: So-called church renovation should be carefully monitored and efforts made to restore more sacred surroundings for worship. As Cardinal Francis George put it, "A change in space, in architecture and in the placement of altars and other liturgical furnishings" has the same effect as a change in language, "which carries and conditions our thinking and evaluating".[29]

Msgr Elliott notes that "in some areas, in Australia for example, church 'renovators' are still destroying our patrimony and alienating people. These renovators are rushing their projects through before the Catholic people discover what is in the revised directives — for example, the location of the tabernacle".[30]

Fr Peter Williams argues, "Perhaps it is time to revisit many of the decisions that were made and effected on our church buildings in attempting to accommodate the demands of the new rites and ask whether what was deemed appropriate in the early stages of the reform is still valid today".[31]

• **Church music**: Bishop Manning describes "some of our present-day Church music and hymns" as "infantile, superficial, banal and utilitarian". Church music, he says, "is meant to uplift minds and hearts to the eternal, to bring true inner feelings and desires before the Lord. It means we do not merely cater for what we like, what we are comfortable with, for we are seeking to glorify the 'Eternal Other'".[32]

The greater use of Gregorian chant, originally called for by Vatican II, has again been strongly recommended by John Paul II and Benedict XVI, along with appropriate settings for the Kyrie, Agnus Dei, Sanctus, Pater Noster and other key parts of the Mass.

Redemptionis Sacramentum

As already noted, *Redemptionis Sacramentum*, published in 2005 at the request of John Paul II, lists common abuses to be eliminated from liturgical celebrations.[33]

The document states that in the event of abuses occurring, "any Catholic has the right to lodge a complaint to the diocesan Bishop or to the Apostolic See ... in truth and charity". However, recent experience indicates that clericalism is still alive and well when lay people dare to point out liturgical abuses to those in authority.

The following are some of the abuses begging to be remedied:

• Making eucharistic bread with additives (such as fruit, sugar or honey) is forbidden.

• The Eucharistic Prayer is to be recited by the priest alone [and that includes the Doxology, "Through Him, with Him ..."]; he may not change the words nor use an unauthorised Eucharistic Prayer.

• The priest must always wear a chasuble over his alb and stole.

• Eucharistic vessels are to be made of precious metal, not glass, earthenware, clay or other breakable materials.

• Pouring the Blood of Christ from one vessel to another is completely to be avoided, and flagons, bowls or other vessels are not to be used in place of chalices.

The rights of the faithful, and reverence during Holy Communion, are emphasised:

• Communicants are free to choose whether to receive on the tongue or in the hand, but if they receive in the hand they must consume the Host in the presence of the minister of Communion.

• People cannot be denied Communion because they choose to kneel or stand.

• The priest must receive Communion before the faithful receive Communion.

• The practice of "self-intinction" (communicants dipping the Host in the chalice) is forbidden.

• The Communion plate should be retained so as to avoid the danger of the sacred Host or some fragment of it falling.

• The Instruction also repeats the rule that children are to make their first Confession before first Communion.

Other norms govern how and when Mass is celebrated:

• Non-biblical texts are not to be used as Mass readings.

• Special Masses for groups are permitted but these groups are not exempt from liturgical norms.

• Cancelling Masses on the pretext of a "fast from the Eucharist" is an abuse to be reprobated.

• Except when the ecclesiastical authorities schedule Mass in the language of the people, priests are always and everywhere permitted to celebrate Mass in Latin.

Emphasis is also placed on distinctive ministries in the celebration of the Liturgy, and the need to avoid diminishing the essential role of the priest:

• Lay people, even religious, seminarians and pastoral assistants, are not to read the Gospel or preach the homily at Mass. (The Bishop may allow lay preaching outside Mass in unusual circumstances.)

• The expression "Special Minister of the Eucharist" is to be replaced by Extraordinary Minister of Holy Communion.

• Extraordinary Ministers are only to be used when needed, not for the sake of "fuller participation of the laity" in the Liturgy.

• Male altar servers remain the norm and are a source of priestly vocations, but the diocesan Bishop may permit female servers.

But such clear directives await implementation in many Australian dioceses. All too often, well-documented complaints from lay people about abuses are disregarded or dismissed with high-handed clericalism by some priests and bishops.

Endnotes

1. Fr Peter Williams, edited text of address given at conferences of the Australian Confraternity of Catholic Clergy and the National Council of Priests, *AD2000*, October 2002, pp 10-11.
2. Monsignor Peter J. Elliott, Interview with Zenit News Service, May 2003.
3. Cardinal Francis George of Chicago, address at conference organised by the Congregation for Divine Worship and the Discipline of the Sacraments to commemorate the 40th anniversary of Vatican II's *Sacrosanctum Concilium*, Vatican, 4 December 2003.
4. Msgr P. Elliott, op. cit.
5. Cardinal Francis Arinze, Interview with *Inside the Vatican*, November 2005.
6. Msgr P. Elliott, op. cit.
7. Mass booklet, Mt Alvernia College, Brisbane, End of Year Mass 2000, 14 November 2000 at San Damiano Centre.
8. Mass booklet, St Saviour's College, Toowoomba, Celebrating Catherine McAuley, "The Dancing Woman", 24 July 2002.
9. Mass booklet, "Dzintari Earth Care Outdoor Mass", quoted in *AD2000*, February 2001, p. 8, "Liturgy: when will the *Statement of Conclusions* make an impact?"
10. Mass booklet, Year of Indigenous People, Aboriginal & Torres Strait Islanders Mass, St Joseph's Cathedral, Rockhampton, 7 February 1993.
11. *The Catholic Leader*, 13 November 1994.
12. *Liturgy News*, September 2000.
13. *Liturgy News*, June 2001.
14. *Liturgy News*, June 2005.
15. *Liturgy News*, September 2005.
16. *Liturgy News*, March 2006.
17. Cardinal George, op. cit.
18. Brisbane Liturgical Commission, "Sacraments of Confirmation and Eucharist", January 1995.
19. Ibid, p. 25.
20. *Sacrosanctum Concilium*, 7 (Flannery Edition, p. 5).
21. Brisbane Liturgical Commission, op. cit.
22. Archbishop Francesco Canalini, address to annual gathering of 120 leaders of

Australian religious congregations, Brisbane, June 2004.
23. Instruction, *Redemptionis Sacramentum*, On Matters to be Observed and to be Avoided Regarding the Most Holy Eucharist, Congregation for Divine Worship and the Discipline of the Sacraments, approved by John Paul II, 19 March 2004, 38.
24. Encyclical Letter, *Ecclesia de Eucharistia* of His Holiness Pope John Paul II to the Bishops, Priests and Deacons, Men and Women in the Consecrated Life and all the Lay Faithful on the Eucharist and its Relationship to the Church, 17 April 2003, 12.
25. Ibid, 15.
26. Bishop Kevin Manning, address at the Thomas More Centre Summer School, Sydney, 9 December 2000.
27. *Redemptionis Sacramentum*, 40.
28. Bishop Manning, op. cit.
29. Cardinal George, op. cit.
30. Msgr P. Elliott. op. cit.
31. Fr P. Williams, op. cit.
32. Bishop Manning, op. cit
33. *Redemptionis Sacramentum*, 184.

Chapter Four

Catholic Schools: Wasted Resources?

What should Australia's bishops do with the Catholic school system if it can no longer fulfil the purpose for which it was established, namely to help form new generations of practising Catholics?

In December 2005, Bishop Geoffrey Jarrett of Lismore told a gathering of Catholic school principals, "The moment is upon us when we cannot take things for granted or just hope for the best. We face the sobering reality of some basic questions, some critical challenges.

"What is, for instance, the real reason for the Catholic Church's engagement in school education? What distinctively makes our schools Catholic, marks them with a mark found nowhere else?"

In this regard, he said, "The most alarming reality which we face, and must do so with eyes wide open", was that "by far the greater part of the students in our schools and their parents" no longer attend Sunday Mass.[1]

Since one recent estimate of Mass attendances among school leavers puts the rate at less than five percent,[2] one is entitled to question the viability of Catholic schools as a means of passing on the faith. It should be noted that Mass attendance correlates with other indicators of belief and practice.[3]

The school systems themselves, drawing billions of dollars of government and private funds and involving the employment of tens of thousands of teachers and administrators, have grown into massive self-perpetuating bureaucracies — at least in the larger cities — of little apparent accountability.

As with other problem areas, the Holy See has issued documents setting out what is required of Catholic schools and their staffs, but with few exceptions, little seems to change. The *Catechism of the Catholic Church* has been with us for over a decade and is listed in many diocesan programs, but its impact at the grass roots seems to have been largely superficial. As far back as 1979, Pope John Paul II issued *Catechesi Tradendae*, which stated clearly what was required of an authentic education in the faith, in both content and method. But its requirements have been honoured more in the breach than in the practice.

While sound religious education texts have been developed in recent years, thanks to the initiative of Cardinal Pell, and are now being used in the Melbourne, Sydney, Armidale, Lismore and Wollongong dioceses, elsewhere the situation is less satisfactory. However, even with the best texts and programs, and the best will in the world, the human resources are insufficient to effect any broad-based recovery, since it is the witness of practising parents, teachers and peers that is crucial to developing and maintaining faith.

In the absence of these, teaching the faith in many Catholic secondary schools today can become a mission impossible.

Not that all bishops even acknowledge a serious problem exists.

In Brisbane, Archbishop Bathersby blessed new school buildings at All Hallows Middle School on 22 May 2006 and lamented the shortcomings, as he saw them, of yesteryear. "My only regret", he said, "is that I learned the Christian message too late, and I hope that you students will learn about it in its fullness much earlier than I did".[4]

Archbishop Bathersby received his primary education at St Joseph's Catholic Primary School, Stanthorpe, and boarded at Nudgee College, Brisbane, for his secondary education.

As the following surveys show, with a few variations here and there according to local circumstances, the levels of belief and practice among students after up to twelve years of Catholic education have been unacceptably low and declining steadily over the past three decades with no sign of any levelling out.

Surveys

In 1992, a statistical survey and analysis, was published by a team including Sr Carmel Leavey OP, the research having been undertaken in 1989. In his preface, Fr Tom Doyle, then Director of the Melbourne Catholic Education Office, admitted that "readers may find the authors' conclusions disturbing" revealing "a religious profile ... which does not provide much consolation".[5]

The study surveyed 266 Catholic girls at three Sydney schools (two Catholic and one Government), representing an approximate socio-economic and ethnic cross-section of the overall Catholic school population. The study found:

• 77 percent affirmed at least a tentative belief in God and Jesus;

• 57-58 percent described themselves as religious or said they have some intention of modelling their lives on the teaching and example of Christ;

• 35 percent had a "positive" self-estimate of their understanding of "the Christian story";

• 13 percent could explain Church teaching on the Incarnation and only two percent could give "an adequate explanation of the Kingdom of God";

• 32 percent said they read religious books;

• 42 percent believed that life after death was certain.

Comparisons with earlier research data were revealing:

• Whereas 48 percent of a similar sample of Catholic students in 1970 thought their work with secular subjects complemented their Christian beliefs, in 1989 the figure was down to 11 percent;

• In the total sample, 90 percent went to weekly Mass in 1970, 63 percent in 1981 and 43 percent in 1989; at one of the sampled Catholic schools the drop was from 96 percent to 37 percent between 1970-1989.

The survey found that "what data we have suggest surprisingly few differences between the State and Catholic school Catholics in religious outcomes".[6] This contrasted with 1966 research by both Hans Mol and Yvonne Robertson which found significantly higher levels of belief and practice among Catholic school Catholics compared with State school Catholics, allowing for other variables.[7]

In other words, according to Sister Leavey's research, up to 12 years of religion teaching in Catholic schools can make little if any difference to belief and practice.

Serving parish priests know this all too well. Interviews are a frequent part of RE homework and priests are accustomed to such questions from Catholic students as "who founded your Church?"

1990 Survey

A far more extensive survey was undertaken in 1990 by the late Dr Marcellin Flynn FMS, with the results published in 1993.[8] These confirmed concerns expressed about the religious character of many Catholic schools in Australia. The survey involved over 6,000 Catholic Year 12 students, their parents and teachers, in New South Wales and the Australian Capital Territory, and followed three earlier studies carried out by Br Marcellin over a period of 20 years.

Br Marcellin was a Senior Lecturer in the Department of Religious Education, Australian Catholic University, Strathfield, NSW, and a recognised leader in his field. He concluded, "A consistent, rapid decline in the religious dimension of the [Catholic] school has taken place over this period [1972-1990] and ... there are no signs that it is about to be arrested".[9]

Of the Catholic students surveyed, only 29 percent thought it very important "to be a practising member of the Catholic Church" and 34 percent said they "feel at home in the Church".[10]

The number attending Sunday Mass according to the survey fell from 69 percent in 1972 to 38 percent in 1990; 53 percent said their parents expected them to attend Mass (compared with 83 percent in 1972).[11]

In the matter of the Catholic Church's moral teachings,

- 70 percent believed it was all right for "people who are not married to live together" (up from 58 percent in 1982);
- 58 percent said abortion was all right if a pregnancy was the result of rape (41 percent in 1982);
- 19 percent accepted the Church's teaching on birth control (27 percent in 1982);
- 20 percent thought sexual intercourse outside of marriage was morally wrong (28 percent in 1972).[12]

Br Marcellin's test of "knowledge of the Catholic faith" consisting of 24 multiple-choice questions had to be shelved because of the students' ignorance of basic religious terminology. "It quickly became apparent," said Br Marcellin, "that Year 12 students were not familiar at all with the theological concepts and language used. (One person asked: 'Who is this person Grace?')".

The average number of correct responses was 11 out of 24, and only one student out of the 6,000 surveyed answered all 24 answers correctly.[13]

Yet such ignorance of the faith was unlikely to cause a parental backlash. "In the case of religious development", said Br Marcellin, "their expectations have shown a marked decline. Parents today do not have high religious expectations of the schools".

Parents unhappy with inferior religious education programs were by 1990 a tiny minority. Only 16 percent were either "concerned" (13 percent) or "very concerned" (three percent) about the teaching of RE at school.[14] This was despite the fact that only 18 percent of teachers in the survey thought students knew the faith well enough.[15]

This is hardly surprising given the inadequacy of the formation of today's Catholic teachers and parents over the past 30 years.

1998 Survey

In 1998, Dr Marcellin Flynn and Dr Magdalena Mok conducted another survey of the religious beliefs and practices of Year 12 Catholic students. It was based on the responses of 8,310 Year 12 students and 1,657 teachers at 70 schools in NSW and the ACT.

The researchers concluded[16], "There is little evidence at present that the drift of youth away from active participation in the life of the Church is about to be arrested ... the alienation of adults and youth from the Catholic Church today remains one of the most pressing pastoral problems of our time".

While the drawing power of Catholic schools remained as strong as ever — with almost 20 percent of the Australian school age population attending Catholic schools — the reasons most students were sent to these schools had little connection with their specific Catholicity. The priorities of Catholic parents (and students) were overwhelmingly secular: vocational, academic, personal and social development being all preferred to religious development.

The survey found that the influence on religious development most cited as important by students — at 71 percent — was "the example and lives of parents". But in answer to the question, "My parents expect me to go to Mass on Sundays", only 34 percent responded in the affirmative, compared with 83 percent in 1972.[17]

This was underlined five years later by the results of a survey commissioned by the Toowoomba Catholic Education Board. This revealed most Catholic parents did not see the religious education of their children as important in their choice of school.[18]

Executive Director of Edmund Rice Education, Queensland, Dr Bill Sultmann, commented, "What the research was saying is that three out of four parents were sending their children to Catholic schools for reasons that didn't correlate highly with the reasons why Catholic authorities were providing schools".

According to Flynn and Mok, as far as students' expectations of Catholic schools were concerned, 11 of the 12 lowest rated expectations proved to be in the religion area, with only 36 percent believing it to be "very important" that students should be taught to bc "guided by the teachings of the Church on moral issues". The figure for teachers on this question was 62 percent.[19]

Sunday Mass attendance, which stood at 38 percent in the 1990 survey, was down to 23 percent in 1998.[20]

Confession — in line with general trends in the Church — had virtually disappeared from the lives of Catholic students. Whereas 37 percent went at least once a month in 1972, this figure was down to three percent in 1998. In 1972, 23 percent went "rarely or never" to confession; in 1998 the figure was 58 percent.[21]

The decline was also evident in basic Catholic beliefs. In 1982, 70 percent believed Jesus to be truly God; in 1998, the figure was 51 percent. In 1990, 59 percent believed Jesus Christ to be truly present in the Eucharist; in 1998, the figure was 51 percent.[22]

The widespread parental apathy regarding the Catholic content of Catholic schools means there is little or no pressure from that quarter on schools or Catholic education offices to measure up. The few parents who do complain are easily fobbed off by officialdom.

Rome may be concerned about the effectiveness of Australia's Catholic schools, but it is powerless unless local bishops bite the bullet and impose themselves on their diocesan educators and bureaucrats.

Perth Survey

In Perth, research in 2004 by Marist Brother, Dr Luke Saker, confirmed that the position in Western Australia was similar to that in the eastern states.[23]

While lecturing in Catholic Studies at Edith Cowan University to undergraduate students wishing to teach in Catholic schools and to teach religious education, Br Saker became aware that these undergraduates, fresh from their year 12 studies at Catholic schools, knew very little of their faith, its doctrines and dogmas, and yet were quick to reject Catholic teachings.

This prompted him to conduct research with first and second year university students who had just completed secondary school and studied religious education in Catholic schools in years 11 and 12.

In his study Dr Saker acknowledged parents, peers, teachers, the media and societal values all play a part in determining students' religious beliefs. But he was interested in finding out what influence the Catholic school and, in particular, senior students' religious education classes played in their religious development and acceptance of the

Church into which they were baptised.

Dr Saker concluded from his research that the majority of Catholic students attending Edith Cowan University completed Year 12 with little or no idea of the basic tenets of Catholicism. The following are a few of the findings from the study:

- 12.1 percent of students agreed or strongly agreed that senior religious education classes were taken seriously by senior students;
- 12.8 percent reported that they attended Mass every Sunday;
- 82 percent stated that they rarely or never went to confession;
- 9 percent saw the use of contraception as sinful;
- 12 percent saw themselves as practising Catholics.

Most students interviewed saw the Church as out of date with contemporary society and, in particular, were highly critical of the Church's moral teachings although they could not state why the Church took such a strong stance on abortion, contraception, euthanasia, in vitro fertilisation and homosexuality.

The major findings of the study were as follows:

- Students did not see that they gained anything from their religious education classes nor did they see these classes assisting them in their religious development.
- Students are rejecting most of the doctrinal teachings of the Catholic Church, for example, Sunday Mass attendance, contraception and divorce and re-marriage.
- Students saw their lived experiences as opposed to the Catholic Church's teachings, especially the moral ones.
- Students saw the Church as out of date with modern society and no longer having any impact on their lives.

Dr Saker's findings were given considerable prominence in *The Record*, Perth's archdiocesan weekly, and these prompted follow-up articles and many exchanges in the letters section.

However, Western Australia's powers-that-be in Catholic education were less than pleased at this public exposé of their failed policies and Dr Saker would subsequently experience the full force of their institutional wrath.

Teachers

Dr Saker's findings underline the problem Catholic schools face in recruiting sufficient numbers of teachers who actually believe and practise the Catholic faith.

This was highlighted in 2002 during an address by Professor Denis McLaughlin of Australian Catholic University (McAuley Campus, Brisbane) at the second national conference of the Association of Principals of Catholic Secondary Schools.[24]

Professor McLaughlin has surveyed the beliefs and practices of students at Australian Catholic University (see chapter five) as well as those of teachers.

"I believe," said Professor McLaughlin, "the vast majority [of teachers] ... have reservations about the contemporary Catholic Church, their employer".

These teachers, he said, along with most Australian Catholics, constituted, a "parallel Church", which largely disregarded the teachings of the "institutional Catholic Church, the Vatican, the Magisterium". In practice, "If they agree with the Church on an issue, it is because the Church position makes sense to them and they actively decide to agree. If a Church teaching does not make sense to them, they will refuse to agree, no matter how often or how clearly or how authoritatively the Church has spoken on it".

As such people see it, he said, this "institution" is more and more out of touch with reality, focusing too much on law, power and authority and too little on service, justice and compassion.

Few young Catholics, he continued, ever consult a priest on any matter. Rather it is Catholic school principals and teachers who are the only "Christ" figures most young Catholics will ever meet. "By default, it is the principal ... and other approachable teachers, who have been given the unofficial leadership of local Catholic communities.

"They are the only God/Church persons the vast majority of Catholics ever meet regularly and the evidence is that Catholic kids do find some religious meaning, not in parishes, but in Catholic schools".

The results of such "religious meaning" were evident. According to McLaughlin, "Data obtained by ACU researchers in Sydney found that 97 per cent of young Catholics abandoned the practice of their faith within 12 months of completing high school".

He continued, "This year [2002], with some of my Masters students, I explored the beliefs and values of Year 12 students. We found the dominant spirituality of the young is more creation-focused than redemption-centred. Most do not believe in original sin, they do not accept that at birth they and others are de facto in a state of alienation from God. Consequently, they do not believe that Jesus' prime mission was a sacrifice for their sins and the sins of others.

"To put it bluntly, the world in which young Australians live is so alien from the world of churchmen as to make formal religion appear irrelevant for them".

As recently as 1970, over half the teachers in Catholic schools were members of religious orders. By 1990, only five percent were, and today there are almost no religious sisters, brothers or priests teaching in Catholic classrooms.

In his 1990 survey, Br Marcellin found of the 95 percent Catholic lay teachers:

- 43 percent thought euthanasia was morally wrong;
- 49 percent thought abortion worse than the birth of an unwanted child;
- 62 percent believed that "Jesus is truly present in the Eucharist";
- 50 percent agreed that "going to Mass on Sunday is important to me".[25]

Br Marcellin concluded that "the religious development of staff may well be one of the most urgent tasks facing administrators in Catholic schools. Many teachers and parents ... referred to the lack of any religious commitment amongst some staff members in Catholic schools, as well as amongst recent graduates of Catholic teachers' colleges".[26]

Professor McLaughlin's research into the beliefs of experienced Australian Catholic principals concluded that "these principals had a practical tolerant view of Catholicism that was more about establishing relationships through service and less on law. All principals privately held views contrary to current Vatican teachings on priestly celibacy, married clergy, female priesthood and artificial birth control".[27]

New Catechetics — the grand con!

There have been several contributing factors to the declining spiritual output revealed by these surveys. One has been the doctrinally shallow "experiential" catechetical approach that has dominated Catholic schools for much of the period since the 1970s. Those who imposed this approach and continue to justify it must be held accountable for the predictable disasters.

A Dominican Sister who believed in and taught the "new catechetics" for many years recalled how she came to recognise its flaws.[28]

"I have taught primary school classes where RE was really just an excuse for creative activities — art, drama, paraliturgies, dance. Meaningfulness equalled fun. And fun equalled a 'successful RE lesson'. The children really liked Religion class and I felt I was getting through to them. But, if pressed, I would have had to admit that they retained very little beyond 'good feelings' and that they had no more than a hazy idea of the religious truths involved".

She later found that secondary school students considered religious education a kind of non-subject.

"It was the subject in which they were least motivated — partly because they saw it as boring and repetitive; partly because it had no intellectual weight and partly because it was not examinable and held no component of academic accountability.

"I did not blame them. They had been fed the ideals of loving, caring and sharing in much the same contexts almost every school day for all those years. Now, eleven years later they were hearing the same messages in scarcely more developed form — 'I am unique', 'people are gifts', 'I'm OK, you're OK.'

"It is no wonder that what was meant to be relevant and meaningful Christianity during all those years began, with the passage of time and repetition, to look like tired platitudes and cliches to these students in Years 11 and 12. They did not realise it, but they had been sold short and I began to realise that in pursuing the 'new catechetics'

I was perpetuating the situation".

Over the same period, Catholic students have been exposed to superficial liturgies in their schools and parishes where the Eucharist is all about the community celebrating itself and more often than not they have been given only the "soft options" of the Gospel. Particularly at secondary school and tertiary level their religious education has become so secularised that students no longer have any realisation of what faith in Christ entails.

These are the kinds of young people applying to teach in Catholic schools. In my experience their reasons for doing so were less to do with the evangelising role of the Catholic Church and more connected with job opportunities and more teacher-friendly environments than those in state schools.

Defective theology

Another factor has been the defective theology picked up after Vatican II by Australian educators studying overseas or from visiting experts — many of them American. These experts' writings in turn have been given prominence in lists of recommended course readings or are even serving as a basis for whole catechetical programs.

A typical example of these is Professor Monika Hellwig of Georgetown University, Washington DC. She has given talks to Catholic educators in Australia since the 1980s and her writings continue to be recommended in diocesan catechetical guidelines for teachers and for courses at Australian Catholic University, which supplies a large number of Australia's Catholic teacher graduates.

One of Hellwig's articles, which had been previously published in the United States, was included in abbreviated form in *The Catholic Leader* (Brisbane) with the headline, "What makes Catholic Schools Catholic?"[29]

Professor Hellwig's article illustrated the substitution process commonly employed in recent theology. In this instance she took the traditional four marks of the Catholic Church, "one, holy, catholic, apostolic" and substituted her own meanings for them.

According to Hellwig, "one" means working for ecumenism and peace among nations. "Holy" means "an attitude of reverence for human life and freedom, gratitude for the good things of creation and a sense of responsibility and focus in life". Being "catholic" is to witness "to social justice and peace by enrolling minority and immigrant students" and teaching "history, social studies and religious knowledge in ways that counteract inbuilt prejudices and hostilities". And being "apostolic" is to reflect "an atmosphere of hope and courage and trust about the future of the human race and of the local society", to inspire "humility and attention towards the cumulative wisdom of the past", and "to find reconciliation and wholeness".

In the same article, Hellwig argued it was no longer the role of Catholic schools to form students "as knowledgeable and committed members of the Catholic Church, who could be trusted to participate in its worship and charitable activities and to conform their lifestyles to its teachings". This aim, it seems, went out the window with Vatican II.

The writings of such people have had a cumulative effect on the Catholic education enterprise since the 1970s, including many of the personnel who staff and administer Catholic education offices.

As a case in point, in February 2004, the Director of the Diocese of Sale Catholic Education Office (Victoria) published a document[30] reporting on the diocese's involvement in an Inter-Diocesan Religious Education Project with the Archdiocese of Hobart and the dioceses of Ballarat and Sandhurst.

Despite their proximity to Melbourne, where an excellent RE text book series for all grade levels had already been produced under the leadership of Archbishop Pell, the Catholic education offices of Sale, Sandhurst and Ballarat consciously chose a different path.

The Sale document gave the purpose of the project as the production of new RE curricula. It added that the RE curriculum of the Archdiocese of Canberra-Goulburn had been chosen as "an appropriate curriculum to serve as a base upon which to build" the new curricula.[31]

Titled *Treasures New and Old*, the Canberra curriculum rests heavily on the method of RE teaching pioneered by the well-known American doctrinal dissenter, Thomas Groome.

Under the heading, "A Well-Groomed Curriculum," the Sale document says, "This curriculum will be based on the Shared Christian Praxis approach developed by Thomas Groome." RE curricula for the dioceses of Wagga Wagga, Wilcannia-Forbes and Parramatta are also tied to Groome's method.

Since this method of teaching calls for critical questioning of the Church's doctrinal, moral, liturgical and juridical tradition it is not surprising that contradictions of Catholic teachings appear in curriculum materials produced by the Canberra CEO for the implementation of *Treasures New and Old*.

The problems begin in the Core Document and Syllabus Statement where the only time the Holy Trinity is designated as Father, Son and Holy Spirit is in an appendix. Otherwise, wherever the Holy Trinity is referred to, it is always as "God: Communion of Love, Source of all Being, Eternal Word and Holy Spirit."

This absence of references to "the Father" and "the Son" when talking about the first and second Persons of the Holy Trinity is not surprising given Groome's espousal of inclusive language for statements of faith.

Regarding the Trinity, he said, "A formula that might more adequately represent our faith in the triune relationship within the Godhead ... is suggested by an inclusive language breviary text which prays 'Glory to you, Source of all Being, Eternal Word, and Holy Spirit'."[32]

In his book *Sharing Faith,* which is a key source for *Treasures New and Old,* Groome refers to the first Person of the Holy Trinity as "God the Father/Mother"[33] while under a section headed "Theological Background for Teachers" of a Stage 5 (Year 11) Canberra Unit Outline we read, "Many images of God emerged within a pre-scientific worldview and antiquated theological models. Today theologians call for the deconstruction of limited metaphors and for the development of new metaphors for God, e.g., God as mother, lover, friend."

A reference book featuring prominently in a Stage 6 (Year 12) Unit is titled *Rome Has Spoken*. These words were first used by St Augustine in referring to the infallibility of the Church in matters of faith and morals. In this instance, the words are used to question this infallibility.

The book carries the subtitle *A Guide to Forgotten Papal Statements and How They Have Changed Through the Centuries* and is edited by Sr Maureen Fiedler and Linda Rabben.

Sr Fiedler, a Loreto nun, was one of the signatories to an advertisement placed in the *New York Times* in 1984 by *Catholics For A Free Choice* (CFFC) which claimed there was no binding Catholic teaching forbidding procured abortion. CFFC is also opposed to Church teaching on contraception and homosexual activity and in more recent years campaigned to have the Holy See expelled from the United Nations.

Regarding papal authority and the way it was exercised by John Paul II, Sr Fiedler says in the introduction to *Rome Has Spoken*, "Within the Church, his doctrinal orthodoxy and repression of dissent have threatened free theological development. His centralisation of church authority has undermined the collegial policies envisioned by Vatican II" (p. 6).

The Stage 6 Unit Outline, which draws extensively on *Rome Has Spoken*, is titled "The Church's Developing Tradition". It claims definitive Church teaching on various questions can be or has changed over time in ways involving a contradiction of received teaching.

Under a section headed "Key Understandings For Students," the Unit Outline is ambiguous about the nature of divine revelation, saying, "The Church must continually grow in faithful response to God's ongoing revelation in time. God's revelation occurred in the past and continues throughout history in world events, in the lives of human beings, in the life of the Church community, etc."

In regard to this, the *Catechism of the Catholic Church* states: "God has revealed himself fully by sending his own Son … The Son is the Father's definitive Word; so there will be no further Revelation after him" (73).

Under a section titled *The Exercise of Papal Authority,* the same Unit Outline claims that "Pope John Paul II and the Congregation for the Doctrine of the Faith (CDF) have moved back to the first Vatican Council's more rigid concept of Papal authority". In fact Vatican II reaffirmed Vatican I's understanding of papal authority, e.g., *Lumen Gentium,* 18.

In a Stage 6 (Year 12) Unit on Sacraments, the writing of another American dissenter, Fr Richard McBrien, is recommended, i.e., "Teacher input on ministry which could come from McBrien, R. (1988), *Ministry.*"

In *Ministry,* Fr McBrien claims that "in the early Church there was no hard-and-fast distinction between clergy and laity," and that this distinction only began to develop "with the establishment of Christianity as the state religion in the fourth century" (p. 33). He then accuses Vatican II of "ambiguity" in its teaching that the ministerial and common priesthoods differ in "essence" and not just in degree (pp. 43-44).

The Unit Outlines also recommend teachers consult the 1994 revised edition of McBrien's book *Catholicism* as a reference when acquiring information for "Key Understandings For Students." However, in 1996, the National Conference of the Catholic Bishops' Committee on Doctrine in the US censured this edition for "certain shortcomings", including his treatment of the Virgin Birth of Jesus, the perpetual virginity of Mary, the ordination of women, his treatment of moral issues such as homosexuality and contraception, and about his tendency to place the teaching of the Church on the same level as the opinion of dissenting theologians.[34]

The Theological Background for Teachers section of a Stage 4 Unit Outline on Sacraments frequently cites from a book by Monika Hellwig. Her book, *Understanding Catholicism* (2002), includes the false claim, "The New Testament really only distinguishes two sacraments — Baptism and Eucharist. Slowly, over time, there grew out of Church tradition the idea of seven sacraments … (Hellwig, 2002, p. 147)."

However, it has been the unbroken teaching of the Church, af-

Thomas Groome (left) and Fr Richard McBrien (right)

firmed in the Catechism, which states (1117), "there are seven that are, in the strict sense of the term, sacraments instituted by the Lord".

In *Catechesi Tradendae*, John Paul II stated that those receiving religious education "have the right to receive 'the word of faith' not in a mutilated, falsified or diminished form but whole and entire, in all its rigour and vigour." He then stressed the importance of not giving young people the idea that the doctrine of the faith is based on "fallible opinions or in uncertainty," but rather that we must "show them" how it is based on the "immovable rock" of the Word of God "who cannot deceive or be deceived."[35]

The methodology adopted to implement an RE curriculum must therefore be consistent with the doctrinal affirmations present in it. John Paul identifies in *Catechesi Tradendae* the criteria that should govern the choice of catechetical methods. "The choice", he says, "will be a valid one to the extent that, far from being dictated by more or less subjective theories or prejudices stamped with a certain ideology, it is inspired by the humble concern to stay closer to a content that must remain intact."[36]

By contrast, in his book *Sharing Faith*, Thomas Groome presents an approach to religious education clearly opposed to the doctrinal element in Catholicism. He states, "Religious educators should approach the faith tradition with a healthy suspicion and, as educators, help people to recognise that 'much that has been proudly told must be confessed as sin; and much that has been obscured and silenced must be given voice'".[37]

Groome structures his method of Shared Christian Praxis to apply what he calls a "hermeneutic of suspicion" to Catholic doctrine, advising against any presentation of the faith in the form of doctrinal propositions.

In *Sharing Faith* he makes clear that any acceptance of revelation as "divinely authoritative doctrine inerrantly proposed as God's word by the Bible or by official Church teaching" has no place in "movement 3 of shared Christian praxis".[38]

Groome's dissent from Church teachings is evident in *Sharing Faith* in regard to the direct succession of the later popes from St Peter, a male-only priesthood, the difference in "essence" between the common priesthood of all the baptised and the ministerial priesthood, and the commissioning of the apostles at the Last Supper to preside at the Eucharist.[39]

Overall, a major defect of Canberra's *Treasures New and Old* is the way its Unit Outlines refer to or reproduce material from the works of dissenters. And while such material is given in the main body of the Outlines, references to the Catechism appear only in the margins.

Despite this, the Core document for *Treasures New and Old,* which praises Groome's RE method of Shared Christian Praxis and recommends his book *Sharing Faith,* carries an imprimatur indicating official Church approval.

With the present miniscule level of faith practice among Catholic school leavers, it is beyond belief that any Australian diocese would have anything whatever to do with Groome's method for its RE curriculum.

A more productive exercise for the CEOs concerned would be to redirect the "hermeneutic of suspicion" away from Church teachings and onto the theories of Thomas Groome and other like-minded gurus. At the same time they should look elsewhere for sounder ways of teaching the faith to young Catholics.

Meanwhile, in some states, comparative religion courses are all but compulsory in Catholic secondary schools.

These knowledge-based studies of Islam, Buddhism and other creeds treat the Catholic faith precisely the same way — just another belief system to be deconstructed and analysed.

While no studies have yet been done, the number of weekly Mass-goers who remove their children from the Catholic system, especially at secondary level, is significant. Many practising parents consider their children's faith better served by attending non-Catholic private schools or the better state schools, and providing catechetical input at home.

Reclaiming Catholic schools for the faith remains of paramount importance. Perhaps it is time the bishops harnessed the energies of the new movements to provide catechesis — following a reliable program such as Cardinal Pell's *To Know, Worship and Love*, in secondary schools, leaving the teachers to the secular subjects. This is one of a number of possible courses of action for improving the situation.

Moment of truth

Thanks to the strenuous efforts of a few bishops, the position has improved marginally in places. But, overall, as the statistics continue to show, the enterprise is failing comprehensively to fulfil its basic purpose of helping to form new generations of practising Catholics.

Merely replicating what is done at non-Catholic private schools and the better State schools hardly justifies the continued existence of large, separate and expensive Catholic systems of education, while the continuance of the word "Catholic" needs to be questioned if there is no longer any significant Catholic identity involved. If circumstances today make it virtually impossible for Catholic schools to fulfil their purpose, perhaps they should retire gracefully or call themselves something else more appropriate and stop pretending to be doing what they are obviously not doing.

One experienced Catholic educator, Br John Moylan CFC, offered the following assessment in 1998:[40]

"Parents, Religious and the Church, who have invested so much in several ways in Catholic schools in the belief that they are necessary for the religious formation of their students, have a right to expect that these schools are giving an authentic, effective Catholic religious education. As their founders have clearly seen, any religious instruction in these schools will not be effective unless the culture of the school speaks to the relationship between the students and God through the Church.

"Indeed, if the culture of the school does not say to its Catholic students that the most valuable thing in life is a living Catholic faith with all that this implies, by that very fact it is giving these students a false education which could be teaching them that religion and the Church are irrelevant; sacramental, liturgical and private prayer is unnecessary; and that one is at liberty to choose one's own moral code.

"Since there is often a strong desire from the parents to have their children in Catholic schools, cannot the schools make certain conditions, about parent involvement, parent education and faith development? If the values of the school are out of harmony with the nonverbals of the home (where religion may come across as marginal, immature or simply unhappy) there will be little hope of the school serving the long-term future faith of the student.

"If there is not change and hard decisions are avoided, could it not be the case that these schools in the not-too-distant future will be Catholic only in name, and be serving a community of only nominal Catholics supplemented by others who choose these schools for a variety of reasons, possibly unconnected with religion?"

The situation Br Moylan feared might come to pass is with us right now and hard decisions still need to be made. Perhaps it is time to go back to the drawing boards. But are there any Catholic leaders willing or able to take such a bold step, one comparable to that taken by the Australian bishops of the late 19th century when they set up separate, self-funded Catholic school systems following the withdrawal of State Aid? Ironically, the return of State Aid since the 1960s has proved to be a mixed blessing for the integrity of the Church's schools.

Endnotes

1. Bishop Geoffrey Jarrett of Lismore, homily in St Carthage's Cathedral on 1 December 2005 at the commissioning of new school Principals appointed for 2006
2. Denis McLaughlin, associate professor, Australian Catholic University, McAuley Campus, Brisbane, address, "Aspiring Towards Authenticity: The Dialectic of Australian Catholic Education", at second National Conference of the Association of Principals of Catholic Secondary Schools, Gold Coast, 2-5 October 2002. Quotes Tacey, 2000, p. 190.
3. See Marcellin Flynn FMS, *The Culture of Catholic Schools: A Study of Catholic Schools 1972-1993*, St Paul Publications, Sydney, 1994.
4. Catholic Archdiocese of Brisbane, Statement by Archbishop John Bathersby, 22 May 2006.
5. Sr Carmel Leavey OP, Margaret Hetherton, Sr Mary Britt OP, Sr Rosalie O'Neill RSJ, *Sponsoring Faith in Adolescence*, E.J. Dwyer, Sydney, 1992
6. op cit, p.155.
7. Hans Mol and Yvonne Robertson, *Dialogue*, Summer, Winter issues, 1968; details quoted in Michael Gilchrist, *Rome or the Bush*, pp. 176-177.
8. Marcellin Flynn, op. cit.
9. Ibid, p. 1.
10. Ibid, p. 103, p. 31.
11. Ibid, p. 111, p. 298.
12. Ibid, p. 312.
13. Ibid, p. 430.

14. Ibid, p. 247.
15. Ibid, p. 257.
16. Marcellin Flynn FMS and Magdalena Mok, *Catholic Schools 2000*, Catholic Education Commission, Sydney, 2002.
17. Ibid, p. 250.
18. *The Catholic Leader* (Brisbane), 23 November 2003, p. 1.
19. Flynn and Mok, op. cit., p. 109.
20. Ibid, p. 245.
21. Ibid, p. 248.
22. Ibid, p. 252.
23. Luke Saker CM, *A Study of 1st and 2nd Year Catholic University Students' Perceptions of their Senior Religious Education Classes in Catholic Schools in Western Australia*, Edith Cowan University, Perth, Western Australia, 2004.
24. McLaughlin, op. cit.
25. M. Flynn, *Culture of Catholic Schools*, pp. 320-321.
26. Ibid, p. 428.
27. *AD2000*, May 2000, p. 3.
28. Sr Mary Augustine Lane OP, "Why the 'new' catechetics is flawed", *AD2000*, May 1991, pp. 8-9.
29. Monika Hellwig, *Catholic School Studies: a Journal of Education for Australian Catholic Schools*, July 1985; *The Catholic Leader* (Brisbane), 23 February 1986.
30. *Bulletin* No. 4, Catholic Education Office, Diocese of Sale, February 2004.
31. Details of the curriculum are available on the Internet at www.ceo.cg.catholic.edu.au
32. Thomas H. Groome, *Language for a Catholic Faith* (Revised and expanded edition), Sheed & Ward, Kansas City, 1995, p. 53.
33. Thomas H. Groome, *Sharing Faith: A Comprehensive Approach to Religious Education and Pastoral Ministry*, Harper, San Francisco, 1991, pp. 442-443.
34. The review of Richard McBrien's book by the US Bishops' Committee on Doctrine was published in the 18 April 1996 edition of *Origins*.
35. Pope John Paul II, *Catechesi Tradendae*, 30, 60.
36. Ibid, 31.
37. Thomas H. Groome, *Sharing Faith*, p. 233.
38. Ibid, pp. 218-219.
39. Ibid, pp. 314, 328, 324, 314.
40. John Moylan CFC, "Catholic schools: do they make any difference?", *AD2000*, August 1998, pp. 8-9 (reprinted from *Catholic School Studies*, Christian Brothers).

Chapter Five

Australian Catholic University: "Theology Transcends the Church"

Central to the difficulties in Australia's Catholic schools has been the lack of sufficient numbers of soundly-educated, practising Catholic lay teachers. Surveys show that a large proportion of Catholic lay teachers do not practise the faith even though many of them are entrusted with teaching it. In this respect, the teachers reflect the condition of the Catholic community as a whole, although one might expect those wishing to teach in Catholic schools and to teach the faith would have a much higher than average level of belief and practice.

A large proportion of Australia's Catholic primary and secondary teachers in the numerically populous eastern states are trained at campuses of Australian Catholic University. This was established in 1991 as a result of the amalgamation of eight former Catholic teachers' colleges in Queensland, NSW, Victoria and the ACT. According to Professor Denis McLaughlin, ACU is "the largest single supplier of teachers for Catholic schools".[1] In Western Australia, Catholic teachers are trained at the University of Notre Dame Australia and the state-sponsored universities.

Since most of those commencing teacher education courses at ACU, after up to 12 years in Catholic schools, are lacking in their knowledge, belief and practice of the faith the obvious solution would be to address this problem before any student teachers graduate.

In practice, however, the content of some courses could quite easily undermine whatever faith students may still have at the outset.

Ex Corde Ecclesiae

John Paul II's Apostolic Constitution on Catholic universities, *Ex Corde Ecclesiae* (1990), remains to be implemented in regard to Australian Catholic University. United action by the Australian bishops to ensure this implementation becomes ever more urgent.

The requirements of *Ex Corde Ecclesiae* are very clear, particularly in regard to the orthodoxy of the theology faculty and their courses.

Under "Identity and Mission", the Pope noted the need for "fidelity to the Christian message as it comes to us through the Church" and for theology courses to be "taught in a manner faithful to Scripture, Tradition, and the Church's Magisterium".[2]

A university's relationship with the Church, he said, must include "a recognition of and adherence to the teaching authority of the Church in matters of faith and morals" and "Catholic members of the university community are also called to a personal fidelity to the Church with all that this implies". Bishops, he added, "have a particular responsibility ... to promote and assist in the preservation and strengthening of their Catholic identity".[3]

Each Catholic university, "makes an important contribution to the Church's work of evangelization" and "all the basic academic activities of a Catholic university are connected with and in harmony with the evangelizing mission of the Church".[4]

The crux of the document was a requirement for "A university established or approved by the Holy See, by an Episcopal Conference or another Assembly of Catholic Hierarchy, or by a diocesan Bishop" to incorporate a set of "General Norms and their local and regional applications into its governing documents, and conform its existing Statutes both to the General Norms and to their applications, and submit them for approval to the competent ecclesiastical Authority".[5]

The General Norms include the following injunctions: "The identity of a Catholic university is essentially linked to the quality of its teachers and to respect for Catholic doctrine. It is the responsibility of the competent Authority to watch over these two fundamental needs in accordance with what is indicated in Canon Law";

"In particular, Catholic theologians, aware that they fulfil a mandate received from the Church, are to be faithful to the Magisterium of the Church as the authentic interpreter of Sacred Scripture and Sacred Tradition"; and

"If problems should arise concerning [a university's] Catholic character, the local Bishop is to take the initiatives necessary to resolve the matter, working with the competent university authorities in accordance with established procedures and, if necessary, with the help of the Holy See".[6]

Catholic identity

The difficulties associated with ACU were evident in a report in *The Australian* newspaper in 2000.[7]

According to the report, a proposal by one of ACU's pro-vice-chancellors (academic) to introduce "some core units that stressed ethics, social justice, spirituality and the more traditional areas of theology and philosophy" prompted "a backlash from staff concerned that the university was becoming too religious and that it would be dragged into the politicised culture war associated with Melbourne's Catholic Archbishop, George Pell".

An approach to one of ACU's pro-vice-chancellors on this report drew a "no comment" response, but no indication that the report itself was inaccurate. It was obvious the vexed question of ACU's Catholic identity remained highly sensitive.

The report noted, "Ask Peter Sheehan [ACU Vice-Chancellor] if the Australian Catholic University is Catholic enough and he candidly admits he'd be putting his head on the chopping block to answer".

This was just two years after the *Statement of Conclusions* — a summary document agreed to by representatives of Australia's bishops during their ad limina visit to Rome in 1998 and by the whole episcopal conference in 1999 — had set out the following requirements for a Catholic university:[8]

"The university itself and the bishops should be attentive to safeguarding the university's Catholic identity. The Catholic university 'makes an important contribution to the Church's work of evangelisation. It is a living institutional witness to Christ and His message, in cultures marked by secularism' (Apostolic Constitution *Ex Corde Ecclesiae* 49).

"The local ecclesiastical authority, who may seek the assistance of the Holy See in the matter, should follow with understanding and with active concern the question of the doctrinal soundness of the theological formation given either in departments of theology in Catholic universities or in other theological centres, called 'theological faculties' in Australia.

"The fidelity to the Church's Magisterium in these institutions and in the publications by their professors will be an important gauge of the Catholic life of the nation today and an influence on it in the future".

Aside from its responsibility to assist in the Church's work of evangelisation — which would justify the word "Catholic" in its name — ACU is basically repeating in its secular courses what is taught at other universities around Australia. If ACU cannot (or will not) adequately carry out what is required by the "Catholic" part of its title, there is little point in its continued existence.

The Ballarat (Aquinas) Campus of Australian Catholic University

Yet this situation is set to go on indefinitely unless ACU is made accountable. Vague, innocuous "mission statements" open to endless interpretations are not the answer. But without episcopal implementation of the *Statement of Conclusions* and *Ex Corde Ecclesiae*, that is the certain outcome.

The report in *The Australian*, however, suggested this is the way ACU would prefer to go, unless persuaded otherwise. Professor Sheehan referred to the incorporation of "mission values" involving such concerns as "social justice, equity, tolerance, and dignity of all human beings". He further noted that ACU should be "unashamed about its Christian ethos and values". None of these shed much light on ACU's specific Catholicity.

It took almost ten years for the US Catholic bishops to produce an implementation document that could gain majority support at the bishops conference and the Holy See's approval. The US bishops endorsed a new set of norms, titled "*Ex Corde Ecclesiae*: An Application to the United States", for Catholic higher education by a margin of 223-31 at their 17 November 1999 conference.[9]

The norms required theologians teaching in Catholic colleges and universities to have a mandatum (or mandate) to teach from the proper Church authority, ordinarily the local bishop. This mandate is described as "fundamentally an acknowledgment by the Church authority that a Catholic professor of a theological discipline is a teacher within the full communion of the Catholic Church". It also calls on Catholic tertiary institutions to declare their Catholic identity clearly in their governing documents.

Something similar is needed from the Australian bishops — and soon.

ACU student survey

A survey of the beliefs, values and practices of ACU students, many of them trainee teachers, was carried out in 1999 by Professor Denis McLaughlin.[10] It found that most of them did not accept Church teaching on abortion, contraception, the Eucharist and women priests. The survey questioned 647 first and final year student teachers at ACU campuses in Sydney, Melbourne and Brisbane.

In his research report McLaughlin said he found no significant differences between first year and final year students. In other words, ACU was having little if any impact for the better on its students' religious beliefs and practices. Students entering ACU religiously impoverished after 12 years in Catholic schools, graduated three or four years later in a similar condition, despite passing in the theology and religion curriculum subjects required for employment in Catholic schools and to be religion teachers.

McLaughlin's study included the following findings:

• One-third of student teachers interviewed believed the bread and wine become Christ's body and blood during Mass. In other words, two-thirds did not, many of whom would later be involved in the sacramental preparation of Catholic children.

• 50 percent said they attended formal worship at least monthly (34 percent weekly or more).

• Two percent accepted the Church's teaching on contraception, with 89 percent indicating it was a personal matter for the couple involved. The figures were the same on acceptance of Church teaching on divorce.

• 14 percent accepted the Church's teaching on abortion, with 37 percent believing it to be justified in extreme circumstances and 35 percent that it was a personal matter for the couple involved. Ten percent accepted the Church's teaching on premarital sex.

• 50 percent of students understood God as meaning the Blessed Trinity.

• 62 percent believed that the priesthood should be open to women.

• 47 percent indicated that Catholic schools should aim to bring children to a knowledge of the Catholic faith, but only 12 percent cited commitment and 16 percent practice of the faith.

These figures, it should be emphasised, are not for average Catholics, but for those who have committed themselves — for whatever reasons — to become Catholic teachers responsible for educating a new generation in the faith, including sacramental preparation in the primary school or inculcating moral values in the secondary school.

It is increasingly evident that these views are permeating the rising generation of young Catholics. In June 2006, a Year 10 student at one of Brisbane's leading Catholic girls' schools was studying the afterlife. Part of a family that has practised the faith for three or four generations in the one parish, she told her parish priest: "Yes, they told us about the Church's teaching on Heaven, Hell or Purgatory, but stress it is entirely up to us if we believe it or not".

ACU course content

Given the scattered nature of ACU's campuses and the large size of the faculties, one cannot generalise about the soundness or otherwise of all religion courses and their recommended readings. But enough materials are available to indicate the existence of widespread problems calling for episcopal action.[11]

My own observations in the 1980s at what is now the Ballarat Campus of ACU and contacts with various ACU students over the intervening years confirm that the following examples are not unusual.

Unit outlines and books of readings for several theology units taught to student teachers at a Sydney campus of Australian Catholic University that came to hand in 2001 certainly raise questions about the general calibre of theology taught at ACU.

The following mind-numbing, often unintelligible passages indicate what student teachers are up against as they struggle to understand their Catholic faith from a position of relative ignorance.

In the Introduction to Theology unit (Theology 102) dissent against "non-dogmatic teachings" is presented as "always a possibility" provided the dissenter has "competence". Fr Richard McBrien's *Catholicism* (1984 edition) was cited as an authority, despite being a flawed guide to the faith, with its favourable presentations of dissenting theologians. It was cautioned against by the Australian bishops at the time it was first published in Australia and the US bishops later acted similarly.[12]

In the same unit, an article by Robert Haight, whose dissenting writings have brought him under Vatican scrutiny, was titled "Why Theology?". It offers the argument that Church authority and doctrine should be downplayed in the interests of ecumenism: "From the standpoint of the church, theology transcends the church. It deals with the whole sphere of reality itself from within the purview of the symbols of Christian revelation. Second, the church itself which is the natural home of theology cannot be restricted to any confessional communion today.

"The premises and values underlying the ecumenical movement, which reach back to the essence of apostolic faith, break open the necessary and legitimate role of authority within any particular Christian tradition ... Christian theology in this situation will attend to the faiths of other peoples and, being influenced by them, reformulate its self-understandings accordingly".

This line of argument runs counter to the teaching of the Vatican document *Dominus Jesus* as to the Catholic Church's particular claims to truth.

Another reading, from *Creating Designs for Theological Reflection*, by Killen and de Beer (1995), encourages students to become in effect home-spun theologians. The lecturer in charge prefaces the reading: "Understanding the basic framework for theological reflection helps us to facilitate it effectively. Learning to use the framework as a resource for developing creative designs for theological reflection is equally important. This chapter presents options and possibilities for designing theological reflection based on each section of the basic framework".

What this has to do with the specific needs of Catholic primary or secondary school religion teachers is not immediately obvious.

In one of the more bizarre readings in the collection, titled "Daughters of the Church: the Four Theresas", Sr Mary Collins OSB equates the stature of dissenting American nun, Sr Theresa Kane — who confronted John Paul II during his first visit to the United States in 1979 with a call for women priests — with that of Mother Teresa of Calcutta, St Teresa of Avila and St Thérèse of Lisieux.

Another unit, titled Studies in Religion and Philosophy (Theology 114) devoted much space to Semitic, Muslim and Indian religious perspectives. Topic 3 in this unit, titled "Religious Pluralism," included a handout from *Dissonant Voices* (1991) which claims that "Vatican II clearly opened the door to a very different way of looking at other religions. For example, *Lumen Gentium*, 8 makes it clear that no longer can the Roman Catholic Church be identified as the sole Church of Jesus Christ" — a misreading of Vatican II's teaching, as reiterated in *Dominus Jesus*.

Next, in an extract from *The Problem of God* by T. William Hall, we read that "critical believers and thinkers in our time might find it more rewarding to look toward newer approaches to the problem of God. These approaches will not focus on the traditional God problem. Rather, attention will be directed to issues of transcendence, as hinted at in religious language, in the depth of the psyche, and even in the rediscovery of experience. It may even be that the creative imagination of men and women in our time will lead to radically new and meaningful affirmations of God hitherto undreamed of".

What the average student teacher would make of this cloudy prose is anybody's guess. But it is unlikely to be the Catholic faith.

A third theology unit, titled Church: A Communion of Believers (Theology 244) includes a book of readings the titles of which are fairly self-explanatory:

"Rethinking Church Models Through Scripture".

"The Community Called Church".

"Empowering God's People at Grassroots Level" in *Redefining Church: Vision and Practice* ed R. Lennan (1995).

"The Recasting of Marian Imagery" in *Hail Mary?: The Struggle of Ultimate Womanhood in Catholicism* (1995).

The theology unit states as its objectives:

"Identify and assess the historical, scriptural and theological developments in understanding ecclesiological paradigms".

"Evaluate the historical and theological significance of such perspectives in ecclesiology as they relate to issues of lay ministry and ecumenism, liberation theology and emerging feminist critiques".

"Identify and critically assess the principal paradigms of the Church that have been proposed by contemporary ecclesiologies in relation to the needs of the local church".

"Identify and critically assess the models of ministry and authority that flow from and express these diverse understandings of the Christian Church".

The feminist influence is very pronounced in some of the units and readings.

In "The Recasting of Marian Imagery" by M. Hammington from *Hail Mary?: The Struggle of Ultimate Womanhood in Catholicism* (1995) it is stated:

"Historical/critical methods, biblical scholarship, and modern social phenomenology contribute to the modern feminist critique of Marian images. The critique, and the current status of women in academics [sic] and in religious ministry, makes for a unique moment in history. In no other era has it been possible for feminist theologians to establish themselves as a significant constituency in the dynamic complexity of the Catholic Church, and therefore lay claim to women's voice in matters of spirituality ... Male theologians have historically exploited popular Marian piety to develop imagery that was useful to patriarchy, solidifying papal power, subordinating women, maintaining moral controls ...

"The three images discussed in this book have brought forth a mandate for change in sexual morality, power structures, and definitions of good and evil. However, Mary represents the position of the official teaching of the Church. The same critiques and recommendations for change could just as easily be focused upon Catholicism. Institutional religious change does not come easily ... Catholic feminists merely seek to reclaim their Church".

Overall, these theology courses with their accompanying readings could lead one to think that:

• The Catholic Church's claims to truth are of less priority than furthering ecumenism.

• The views of theologians can be equated with those of the Magisterium.

• The Church's hierarchical character should be understood in natural rather than supernatural terms.

• A liberal, feminist, politically correct, line of thinking is the way to go for the Church — and for future Catholic teachers.

• What the Church officially teaches, as set out in the *Catechism of the Catholic Church*, need not be emphasised or defended.

• Church teachings are often ambiguous and open to debate for Catholics.

• Students need to learn the theological ropes so as to be able to critically "reflect" on these teachings. Thomas Groome's "hermeneutic of suspicion" comes to mind.

Lecture notes

From another vantage point have come extracts from student notes taken down during a series of lectures in theology at a Sydney campus of Australian Catholic University in 2005.[13]

The following are paraphrased understandings of what the lecturer was conveying as well as some direct quotes.

• God the Father should also be recognised as "God the Mother".

• Regarding the Asian Tsumani: "It was not a mini warning. If we were to experience such a thing, it would happen in the Vatican City. I would love to see all those Monsignori floating around".

• The Eucharist is essentially a meal shared by an assembly.

• A priest's job is to help people become whole selves and grow in maturity, not to get them to attend Mass or go to confession.

• Celibacy should be scrapped from the Church — "it isn't realistic".

• Women should be encouraged into the priesthood.

• The Australian Catholic University was established so that religious education could be "relevant" and "modern".

• Australian parents would consider their child's teacher as the person "in-control" of Church teachings more so than priests, bishops and Pope.

• Marriage is out of fashion: "It has never survived the Industrial Revolution and won't." The Church should have nothing to do with marriage.

• "Eucharist has nothing to do with transubstantiation"; it becomes the Body of Christ because we are taking it and we are the Body of Christ.

• The tabernacle should be removed so that people became the focal point.

• The concept of original sin was influenced by St Augustine's "dislike of sex".

• Original sin is "not in the Bible".

• The lecturer had "lots of reservations" regarding the church counselling pregnant women considering abortion.

• Regarding the Sacrament of Penance, "I personally like the Third Rite and know people who still use it".

Overall, a student who completed this theology unit at Australian Catholic University would conclude from the lectures and discussions:

• The Church's foundations of truth ought to be downplayed in the interest of progressive beliefs.

• The views of theologians, lecturers and students are equivalent to those of the Magisterium.

• A liberal, feminist, politically correct, line of thinking is the way to go for the Church and for educators.

• What the Church teaches in the *Catechism of the Catholic Church* — and even in the Scriptures — does not need to be defended and can be filtered out and translated to suit a more modern way of thinking.

• Church teachings are often unclear and open to debate or personal interpretation.

ACU faculty

Without wishing to generalise about ACU's religion faculties as a whole — having known personally several lecturers of impeccable orthodoxy — it is clear that some at least have had difficulties with Church teachings, to judge from their writings and course outlines.

In a 1997 article titled "A New Relationship Between The Ministerial and Baptismal Priesthoods", Dr Gideon Goosen, Associate Professor of Theology and Religious Education at the ACU in Sydney, proposed "a new conceptual framework" with which to understand the nature of the ministerial priesthood.[14]

"All ministries are sacraments," says Goosen, and in future, "the possible pool of candidates" for ordination will be "broadened to include the married and women".

As to the origin of the Seven Sacraments, Goosen asserts, contrary to the *Catechism of the Catholic Church*, that "the seven sacraments ... do not all go back to the historical Jesus".

A prescribed book for several courses in Christian Ethics run at the ACU in Sydney since 1995 is titled *Freedom and Purpose: An Introduction To Christian Ethics*. It is written by Robert Gascoigne, an Associate Professor and Senior Lecturer in the Department of Theology and Philosophy at the ACU in Sydney.

In referring to mortal sin, Gascoigne says it should be understood in terms of a "fundamental option," meaning "a state of personal being which rejects the love of God and neighbour at the deepest and freest core of the person".

Gascoigne adds: "We can sin by freely doing wrong in individual actions, without these individual actions necessarily reversing the whole thrust and meaning of our lives". "Traditional" Church teaching on mortal sin, is, he says, "implausible".

However, in his 1983 Apostolic Exhortation *Reconciliatio et Paenitentia*, John Paul II rejected the theory of fundamental option as presented in Gascoigne's book. Mortal sin, he says, cannot be reduced to a "fundamental option" whereby it cannot be committed through a single action "in which one freely and consciously chooses to act contrary to God's commandments in a grave matter".

Gascoigne further claims that "the magisterium has no unique competence or authority in the detailed knowledge required for developing specific moral norms", even if "the moral teaching of the magisterium calls for respect and serious reflection by members of the Church, and should only be departed from after conscientious and self-critical consideration of the relevant question".

Yuri Koszarycz, Senior Lecturer in Religion Studies within the School of Theology at the ACU in Brisbane (McAuley Campus), had a personal home page on the website of the ACU, which he dedicated to Fr Charles Curran, an American theologian whose licence to teach theology at a Catholic university was withdrawn some years ago because of his unorthodox views.

In one article on his web page titled "Women And The Church", Koszarycz stated, "Given our modern understandings of justice and equality, the Church in maintaining a significant distinction between hierarchy and laity and the excluding [of] women from priesthood, radically affirms women's inferior position among the people of God".

After recalling how Thomas Groome has asserted that women were not excluded from presiding at Eucharistic liturgies in the early Church, Koszarycz adds that while "the issue of women's ordination is a vital one it is not yet being adequately addressed by those in authority" and that "full membership by men and women in regard to priestly offices and functions [is] necessary".

Shortly after the website for the monthly religious journal *AD2000* was set up, with a number of reports on ACU's theological problems, representation was made by ACU to have these reports removed from the website.[15] This attempt at censorship was rejected and no further action ensued from ACU, but it highlighted the mind-set of those who prefer to shoot the messenger rather than be accountable for any failings or take appropriate action to address them.

Alternatives

Given the above doubts about the adequacy of Australian Catholic University as a religious educator of Catholic teachers, the obvious question is what needs to be done?

Peter Sheehan, the Vice-Chancellor of ACU, sought to address the issue of ACU's Catholic identity in an article in *Australasian Catholic Record* in 2002.[16]

Dr Sheehan wrote, "This is not an argument that in any way challenges the relevance of Catholic tradition. Rather it asserts the primary importance of tradition but requests a careful statement of a Catholic Mission of higher education where the question of Catholic identity should be addressed in ways whereby students and staff can engage mutually in the fostering of a true commitment to the Catholic tradition of intellectual life".

While reasonable enough as far as it goes, this statement does not come to grips sufficiently with the realities outlined in this chapter, the requirements of the *Statement of Conclusions* and the fact that many ACU students will become Catholic teachers. If ACU's role as a university means it cannot adapt sufficiently to the needs of the Catholic school system, perhaps it should opt out of teacher education altogether and hand over this responsibility to other bodies geared more specifically to this task.

If the bishops cannot unite in ensuring implementation of *Ex Corde Ecclesiae* and the *Statement of Conclusions*, perhaps individual bishops should consider setting up their own separate systems of accreditation to plug any holes left by particular ACU campuses. A teaching diploma or degree from ACU may not guarantee a given individual is equal to the task of forming the next generation in the Catholic faith.

The problems with ACU have been partly offset by the establishment of other Catholic tertiary level institutes in recent years, including Notre Dame Australia in Fremantle, Western Australia, and later a sister campus in Sydney, as well as the John Paul II Institute for Marriage and Family in Melbourne and Campion College in Sydney. However, these bodies collectively enrol only a small fraction of the numbers attending the ACU's campuses.

Certification at some of these centres — including for those who have completed their professional degrees at secular universities — to teach RE in Catholic schools, or even fully-fledged diplomas or degrees in education, would serve as an alternative means of accrediting Catholic teachers. A step in the right direction has been taken by the Sydney Catholic Adult Education Centre which now provides accreditation for practising teachers to teach religious education in schools in the Archdiocese of Sydney.

Endnotes

1. Denis McLaughlin, Australian Catholic University survey of students, 1999, cited in *AD2000*, May 2000, p. 3.
2. John Paul II, Apostolic Constitution on Catholic Universities, *Ex Corde Ecclesiae*, 15 August 1990, 3.
3. op. cit., 27, 28.
4. op. cit., 49.
5. op. cit., General Norms.
6. Ibid.
7. *The Australian*, 18 October 2000.
8. *Statement of Conclusions*, 55-59.
9. "US Catholic Universities: Bishops endorse tighter controls", *AD2000*, February 2000, p. 5.
10. McLaughlin, op. cit..
11. Copies of course outlines and readings made available by ACU students, cited in *AD2000*, March 2001, pp. 8-9.
12. Michael Gilchrist, *Rome or the Bush*, pp. 268-272.
13. Lecture notes made available by ACU students in 2005.
14. Eamonn Keane, "How orthodox are Australian Catholic University professional staff?", *AD2000*, October 2000, p. 11.
15. Copies of correspondence at National Civic Council.
16. Peter W. Sheehan, "Some Special Challenges Facing a Contemporary Catholic University", *Australasian Catholic Record*, April 2002.

Chapter Six

Beliefs and Practices: the Lost Sheep

While the Catholic Church has been the largest single denomination in Australia for the past 20 years, at about 27 per cent of the national population, the percentage of its membership that believe and practise what their Church teaches continues to fall.[1]

Those who have held the reins over this period may attribute the decline to forces completely outside their control such as the inroads of secularism and family breakdown. However, for decades they have had control of a vast Catholic school system with the opportunity to ensure that no young Catholic from Prep to Year 12 is left in any doubt about the Church's teachings and how they can be justified.

Most Australian Catholics have attended Catholic schools since the late 1960s, but as indicated in earlier chapters, the Church's authorities and educators have squandered their opportunity to build up the faith of young Catholics. They have failed to prepare teachers of the faith adequately and overseen the design and implementation of shallow and defective religion programs. It is they who need to be held to account for the predictably dismal spiritual results we see today.

In 1989, in his observations on the condition of Catholicism, Dr Michael Mason, Redemptorist and sociologist, stated that approximately one million practising Catholics had been "lost" to the Church in the fifteen years between 1966 and 1981. He added, "Projections for several large dioceses show that by the mid-90s the number of active diocesan clergy in parishes will be a third to a half fewer than in 1976".[2]

According to B.A. Santamaria, the poorly handled liturgical reforms after Vatican II were a major factor in this decline. "The arrogant and brutal destruction of the 'old' Mass", he remarked, "has been followed by a limp and occasionally desacralised successor. The sense of mystery has been replaced by chattering friendliness on the part of the congregation within the precincts of the church, which rarely displays any of the traditional Catholic reverence for the Blessed Eucharist, raising the question of how much real belief in the Real Presence remains".[3]

This loss of faith in the Real Presence (along with banal, trivilalised liturgies) has been symptomatic — indeed one of the major causes — of a wider decline in Catholic belief and practice.

The final result, Mr Santamaria added, "is that many, with increasing seriousness, ask the question, 'Is this really the Catholic Church to which we have pledged our conviction and our resultant loyalty? Or has it become something else, in the course of an evolution which even so great a Pope as John Paul II, is incapable of reversing?"[4]

Following release of Pope John Paul II's encyclical *Veritatis Splendor* in October 1993, Santamaria wrote, "The crisis must if possible be ended, or the Church will cease to exist as a Church of the masses".[5]

John Paul stated his specific objective as addressing "a new situation [which] has come about within the Christian community itself, which has experienced numerous doubts and objections ... with regard to the Church's moral teachings. It is no longer a matter of limited and occasional dissent, but of an overall general and systematic calling into question of traditional moral doctrine".[6] The Pope called this situation "a genuine crisis".[7]

This crisis of dissent has also included a crisis of practice among Catholics.

In 1971, Dr Hans Mol's book *Religion in Australia* quoted two alternative figures for the weekly religious practice of Catholics in the decade of the sixties. One source stated that 60 percent of those who identified themselves as Catholics went to Mass every Sunday. The Gallup Polls produced lower figures, between 54-55 percent.[8]

By 1986, in the Melbourne Archdiocese — fairly typical of the rest of Australia — approximately 26 per cent went to Mass each week. Five years later, the level had fallen to 22 per cent and by 1993 it was 20.5 per cent. Within these average figures there were significant variations from parish to parish and according to age and ethnic identity.[9]

The disproportionate number of older people at Mass has meant there is an inbuilt decline, since the rate of attendance is much lower in the younger age groups, with few school leavers continuing to attend.

B.A. Santamaria predicted — accurately — that this could lead to an average attendance rate of around 15 per cent by the end of the 1990s. He wrote, "If the factors which have led to the present situation have been effectively countered, 15 percent constitutes a sufficient base for the regeneration which is indispensable. If, however, the present chaos, particularly in the field of belief, persists, the Church will simply fragment into a sect".[10]

1996 Survey

During November 1996, in what was the largest project of its kind in the Church's history in Australia, 250,000 Catholics in about 400 parishes were asked to fill out one of four different survey forms distributed during Masses. This represented about one-third of the pollsters' estimate of 750,000 Australian Catholics at weekly Mass.[11]

The project, known as the Catholic Church Life Survey (CCLS), was conducted under the auspices of the Australian Catholic Bishops Conference and paralleled the National Church Life Survey which encompassed all Christian denominations and coincided with the 1996 Commonwealth Census.

Subsequent analysis of the CCLS returns found that 63 percent of those aged 15-39 who attended weekly Mass accepted the central article of Christian faith that "There is one God, Father, Son and Holy Spirit," while 83 percent of those over 60 did so. Of those aged over 60, 80 percent affirmed that the consecrated bread and wine "truly become the sacred Body and Blood of Christ," but only half of those under 40 did so.

Under the category of "The Faith Experiences and Beliefs of Church Attenders", Catholics, compared with the other 21 Christian denominations surveyed, were ranked second last on the proposition: "Strongly agree Christ was God, human, rose from dead".

On the question of abortion, only 36 percent of Mass attending Catholics agreed with the statement "Abortion should never be permitted", while 10 percent endorsed the view that "Abortion should be more generally available".

Responses to the other questions were of this level of acceptance of Church teachings, yet these were of the small percentage (in 1996 down to 18 per cent nationally) of regular Mass-attending Catholics. The belief level among the non-attending majority would certainly have been lower.

2001 Survey

The next National Church Life Survey took place in 2001, with around 435,000 church attenders from over 7,000 parishes and congregations in 19 denominations participating. The results of other surveys conducted by individual churches between 1996 and 2001 were taken into account.

Compared with 1996, Catholic Mass attendance had declined from a national average of 18 per cent to around 15 per cent.[12]

Bob Dixon, Director of the Pastoral Projects Office of the Australian Catholic Bishops Conference, provided an analysis of data from the 2001 National Attendance Count conducted by the Pastoral Projects Office as well as from the 2001 National Church Life Survey.[13]

"The current state of church attendance among Australian Catholics," said Dixon, "poses a significant challenge for the Catholic Church in Australia". On a typical weekend, an average of 765,000 people attended Mass in Catholic parishes and other centres around the country, representing about 15.3 per cent of the Catholic population of 5,001,624 according to the 2001 Census.

The attendance figure was based on a head count conducted in all parishes on each of the four weekends of May 2001. In addition, according to the National Church Life Survey, about 87 per cent of people at Mass on a given weekend attend every week or almost every week, so that only 13.3 per cent of all Catholics actually fulfilled their

Sunday Mass obligation.

"This is only the most recent part of a steady decline which began at least 25 years ago", said Dixon. The latest figures "provide a stark contrast with the 1950s, when the weekly attendance rate for Catholics may have been as high as 60 to 65 per cent".

Dixon added, "An examination of the age profile of Mass attenders strongly suggests that the steady fall in attendances will continue for some time to come".

This is because a disproportionate number of Mass attenders come from the older age categories, with, for example, rates of 27.4 per cent (down from 33.5 per cent in 1996) for those aged 60-64 and 31.1 per cent (down from 36.4 per cent) for the 65-69 category.

Among younger Catholics, only 6.8 per cent of those aged 20-24 attended regularly (down from 7.2 per cent in 1996) and 5.6 per cent of the 25 to 29 group (down from 7.0 per cent) attended.

An inevitable consequence of the low attendance rate of Catholics in their twenties, said Dixon, is that there will probably be further large falls in the number of children attending Mass in the next few years, "since almost all children who attend Mass go with at least one of their parents. If fewer people in the generation which is beginning, or will soon be beginning, to have children are Mass attenders, there will also be fewer children at Mass".

In 2001, 11.4 per cent of children aged 0-14 were at Mass (down from 14.8 per cent in 1996), while for those aged 15-19, the figures were lower still.

Such a minuscule level of attendance among school age Catholics raises questions about the wisdom of continuing with school Masses, where invariably all present line up for Communion, whether or not they have fulfilled their Sunday Mass attendance obligation. But priests objecting to this situation receive little if any episcopal backing.

The 2001 National Church Life Survey included a random sample of 261 Catholic parishes from about 1,400 across Australia. From the 255 parishes in the sample which actually took part, 78,255 completed questionnaires were received.

Some versions of the questionnaire contained a series of questions about central Catholic doctrines and moral teachings and were completed by 10,805 Catholic attenders from the national random sample of parishes.

The three belief items dealt with views about the virgin birth, the Eucharist and the nature of God, while the morality items concerned abortion and pre-marital sex.

Acceptance of the Virgin Birth among Mass attenders was broadly similar across age groups, ranging from 73 per cent for those aged 18-24 to 81 per cent for those aged 56 or over.

The differences between age groups were more pronounced in the case of belief in the Eucharist truly being the Body and Blood of Christ. Only 46 per cent of 15-17-year-old Mass attenders accepted this doctrine, whereas 81 per cent of those aged over 56 did so. In between these groups the level of belief rose with age.

Belief in God as the Holy Trinity again reflected age differences, with 51 per cent of 15-17-year olds accepting it, increasing to 78 per cent for over 56-year-olds.

Generational differences were also marked in the case of the Church's moral teachings.

In regard to premarital sex, only 20 per cent of Mass attending 15-17-year-olds considered this to be always morally wrong, 27 per cent of 18-24-year-olds thought so, and this rose to 65 per cent for those over 56.

In the case of abortion, 31 per cent of those aged 15-17 thought it always morally wrong, 34 per cent of those aged 18-24 did so, while the figure rose to 50 per cent for those aged from 40-55 and 64 per cent for those aged over 56.[14]

A significant percentage in all age groups thought abortion could be justified in extreme circumstances.

Within each of these age groupings, Bob Dixon found variations according to the level of parish involvement, with the highest level of acceptance of the Church's doctrinal and moral teachings among "parish involved Catholics", a lower level for "Sunday Catholics" and lower still for "intermediate Catholics" (irregular Mass attenders).

This confirmed the link between Mass attendance and other indications of belief and practice.

But if acceptance of the Church's doctrinal and moral teachings is already low among the 15 per cent of regular Mass attenders, it is safe to assume it is far lower among the remaining 85 per cent who do not attend regularly — if at all.

Another Mass count was taken in May 2006, with the National Church Life Survey and the Commonwealth Census due to be conducted later in the year. The results of these will take some time to collate and analyse.

Given the inbuilt age/attendance rate nexus noted earlier, the decline in Mass attendances will have continued over the past five years. If the average national figure was 18 percent for 1996, and 15 percent for 2001, the figure for 2006, barring some sort of miracle, is likely to be around 12-13 percent or less. Bob Dixon's prediction that "the steady fall in attendances will continue for some time to come" is likely to be confirmed when all the statistics have been analysed.

Endnotes

1. Bob Dixon, Director Pastoral Projects Office, Australian Catholic Bishops Conference, "Mass attendance trends among Australian Catholics: a significant challenge for the Catholic Church", *South Pacific Journal for Mission Studies*, No 28, July 2003, pp. 3-8.
2. *AD2000*, June 1989, p. 11.
3. *AD2000*, June 1989, p. 3.
4. Ibid.
5. B.A. Santamaria, "The state of Catholicism after *Veritatis Splendor*", *AD2000*, February 1994, pp. 5-8.
6. *Veritatis Splendor*, par 4.
7. *Veritatis Splendor*, par 5.
8. Hans Mol, *Religion in Australia*, Nelson, 1971.
9. B.A. Santamaria, op. cit.
10. Ibid.
11. P. Kaldor et al, *Taking Stock: A Profile of Australian Church Attenders*, Openbook Publishers, Adelaide, 1999; "Catholic Church Life survey's shock findings", AD2000 Report, *AD2000*, December 1999-January 2000, p. 7.
12. Bob Dixon, op. cit.
13. Ibid.
14. Ibid.

Chapter Seven

John Paul II's Impact Undermined

Pope John Paul II's pontificate from 1978 to 2005 was one of the longest in the Church's history. In Australia, its impact was felt during two unforgettable visits in 1986 and 1995, as well as through a succession of encyclicals, letters and addresses.

However, in many places the Pope's impact on the grass-roots was lessened due to the opposition or lack of co-operation of a number of strategically placed individuals and Church organisations with a different agenda. At the same time, many bishops seemed reluctant to take remedial action even in the face of public doctrinal dissent.

At the time of his election in October 1978, John Paul II inherited a Church racked by division in the wake of the Second Vatican Council. The Pope sought to restore order by clarifying what the Council actually taught — as distinct from the free-floating "spirit of Vatican II" so cherished by the Church's ageing progressives.

Several of the Pope's encyclicals and authoritative publications such *Veritatis Splendor* (The Splendour of Truth), the *Catechism of the Catholic Church* and *Ordinatio Sacerdotalis* (On the Priesthood) drew particular opposition in Australia, as did others of John Paul's documents.

Veritatis Splendor

John Paul II's encyclical *Veritatis Splendor* was released on 5 October 1993 having taken six years to complete.

In a talk at the Thomas More Summer School in February 1994, Bishop Kevin Manning (then of Armidale) provided an outline of the encyclical.[1]

John Paul, he said, had observed a general and systematic calling into question of traditional moral doctrines. The Pope insisted that these could be known, and were not the product of opinion polls or created by individual consciences.

The purpose of the encyclical, said Bishop Manning, was not merely to warn against errors but "to proclaim anew the message of Christian freedom, for at the heart of this message is the conviction that only in truth does our freedom become truly human and responsible".

But while Bishop Manning and other bishops were promoting and explaining the encyclical, some prominent or influential Catholics were attacking it.

Morris West, well-known Catholic author, and a regular critic of John Paul II's pontificate, contributed two long articles in *The Australian*. In one of them, West professed to find "something quite chilling in the tone of the theological arguments presented in the encyclical, in the constant use of the male collective 'mankind' and the catch-all labels for theological error". He described the encyclical as "a peremptory imposition of authority".[2]

Fr Michael Kelly SJ, at the time publisher of *Eureka Street* and the then recently-launched *Australian Catholics*, contributed a feature article to *The Canberra Times*. The encyclical, he said, had "not only to be proclaimed but also to be *received* (Fr Kelly's emphasis) by the universal Church". As far as Australia's likely "reception" of the encyclical went, said Fr Kelly, the Church in this country had become a "pluralistic entity".[3]

Many Catholic feminists, he said, "will see the encyclical as yet another instance of the deafness of their Church's male celibate law-makers to anything beyond the experience of those same males".

Fr Kelly's views were also reported in *The Australian*. He said that there would be many "dedicated and deeply committed Catholics" who would feel aggrieved by the encyclical. "It will not resolve the matter because a lot of people in the Catholic Church will not feel that they are being heard".[4]

The Provincial of the Jesuit Order, Fr William Uren SJ, took the contrary side against Bishop George Pell (then a Melbourne auxiliary bishop) in a *Four Corners* special on the encyclical. The Pope, said Fr Uren, "needed to present better arguments". He was later reported in *The Australian* as calling the encyclical "a step backward", "a retreat into the ecclesiastical ghetto" and the beginning of a more "totalitarian" image for the Church.[5]

B.A. Santamaria, responded to these attacks saying it afforded him "no pleasure publicly to criticise the leader of the most influential religious order in this country, as it is throughout the world. But if a Provincial believes that he has the right publicly to contradict the Pope, he can hardly complain if his own statements are brought under equally public scrutiny".[6]

Mr Santamaria continued, "The ABC's session, *Four Corners* (October 11), which was clearly set up to demonstrate the divisions in Catholic ranks, provided first-class documentation as to where the land actually lay. Bishop Pell did not shirk the task of explaining, defending, and insisting on the binding force of the encyclical. Unfortunately, his prime antagonist was a Jesuit in open conflict both with the Bishop and the Pope.

"In a following interview in *The Australian* (13 October), Fr Uren stated that the encyclical was the product of an 'authoritarian' coterie surrounding the Pope, and that the Papacy should open itself up to other intellectual positions. The statement was both patronising and ill-informed".

Mr Santamaria then turned his attention to Fr Kelly. "An even more practical issue arises," he said, "from the publication of a new Catholic illustrated journal *Australian Catholics* by Fr Michael Kelly SJ, in the light of his reaction to the encyclical — which was identical with that of Fr Uren and repeated on several occasions".

He noted Fr Kelly's statement that "all expenses [for publishing *Australian Catholics*] will be met by resources from the participating groups". These groups comprised the St Vincent de Paul Society, Pontifical Mission Societies, Australian Catholic Health Care Associations, the Catholic Church Property Insurance Co, and the Jesuits.

"One perhaps may disregard," said Santamaria, "the simple question of the propriety of the St Vincent de Paul Society's diverting money collected for the poor, and of the Pontifical Mission Societies that collected for the missions, to any extraneous purpose. It is significant, with the exception of the little which general advertising may contribute, that $500,000 a year is the extent of the subsidy given by the Catholic Church to a publication issued by an Order which, through its representatives, has led the Catholic attack on the encyclical and its authority".

Getting to the heart of the problem in today's Church, Santamaria remarked, "It is almost certain that this decision is simply the result of the habitual administrative weakness of the Catholic system which permits such a scandalous result to eventuate".

Fr James Murray, a Sydney Anglican priest and religion writer for *The Australian*, was one of the participants in the *Four Corners* program on *Veritatis Splendor*.[7]

He commented that the Pope deserved "better than the disloyalty of some Catholics" and in a perceptive analysis of the state of the Catholic Church in Australia, he said the *Four Corners* program revealed "there are already two teams, one obedient to the teaching authority of the Church, and the other questioning the right of the Pope and the Bishops to present a coherent, if unpopular, system of morals ... The program became the evidence that the split is real".

Fr Murray concluded, "The *Four Corners* program offers a warning to all the Churches that the crisis in authority can even affect an institution as ancient as the Catholic Church. The encyclical is likely to separate the sheep from the goats, or even the shepherds from the sheep".

Catechism

Released at about the same time as *Veritatis Splendor*, and drawing similar criticisms, was the *Catechism of the Catholic Church*.

Almost ten years earlier, the 1985 Extraordinary Synod of Bishops in Rome had recommended the production of a universal Catechism. John Paul II established a Commission the following year headed by Cardinal Joseph Ratzinger to prepare the Catechism which then went through a succession of drafts, involving the world's bishops and hundreds of theologians. The first edition, in French, materialised in 1992.

One member of the Commission, Archbishop William J. Levada of Portland, Oregon (now Cardinal Ratzinger's successor as Prefect of the Congregation of the Doctrine of the Faith), commented during the drafting phase that Catholics concerned about the Catechism's content would be "pleased with the work of the Commission". The Catechism, he said, "will be of assistance in developing the really comprehensive materials that we need to have if we're going to have a truly educated next generation of Catholics, if we're going to have people who know their faith and are able to put that faith into practice".[8]

However, for many of those who had overseen the emergence of the "new catechetics" since the late 1960s, and the subsequent spread of religious illiteracy among young Catholics, such a development was anathema.

In the lead-up to the Catechism's release, groups of theologians and catechetical writers around the world did their utmost to discredit it. The aforementioned Thomas Groome of Boston College, a centre where many of Australia's Catholic educators had been formed in the new catechetics, reacted negatively at the very idea of a Catechism.[9]

In Sydney, a series of talks took place at a two-day clergy in-service seminar which coincided with the official launch of the Catechism in Australia on 22 June 1994. These talks were later included in a book which was designed "to assist those engaged in the use and application of the Catechism".[10]

The talks were presented by theologians involved in the education of future priests at the Catholic Institute of Sydney and, later these same theologians would be running Catechism in-service sessions for Catholic teachers.

Of the ten contributors dealing specifically with the contents of the Catechism, only one, Fr Clement Hill, was consistently favourable.

The overriding theme was that the Catechism had failed to defer to the "cream" of modern theologians and its shortcomings needed "correction" by local catechisms, no doubt to be produced under the supervision of Australia's own experts.

Fr David Coffey, one of the speakers, was involved in controversy several years earlier over his teaching on the Resurrection which led to Vatican intervention.

According to Fr Coffey, the Catechism was effectively fundamentalist for presenting the doctrine of original sin "in an extremely literal way, based ... on the historical existence of the first parents, their sin (to which they were tempted by the Devil, whose personal existence is affirmed) and a historical contraction from Adam by all human beings through propagation".[11]

He claimed that the "culture" of the Catechism "has serious problems of its own, which is why it has been left behind by modern theology" while its "sexist language" would "only offend and deter the an-

Pope John Paul II meets with some Australian bishops

ticipated lay readers". They would also "be baffled by the scholastic and non-pastoral approach which they are not likely to have encountered before".

Dr Neil Ormerod said the Catechism did not, "apart from a few very limited references, seek to make any contact with contemporary theological researches or even, in the sections I have read, with contemporary culture". He considered "a large task of enculturation" still needed to be done and that the Catechism "should not be seen as a 'stand alone' document".[12]

Fr Richard Lennan argued the Catechism had made "no attempt to draw from the accumulated wisdom of the various inter-denominational dialogues which have taken place over the last generation"[13] and was reluctant to "highlight a developmental approach to the Church", with "the Spirit's role in helping the Church to grow, rather than simply to persevere ... often left underdeveloped".

"A greater acknowledgment of the history of development," Fr Lennan said, "would have allowed the Catechism to be an encouragement for a Church struggling to respond to contemporary issues such as feminism. In addition, a more developmental understanding would have enabled the Catechism to demonstrate how the Church can respond to the challenges raised by contemporary exegesis, fundamental theology and hermeneutics. As it is, the idea of Jesus bequeathing the Church a definite and immutable structure, is vulnerable to the insights of these disciplines".

Sr Marie Farrell RSM concluded her paper on "The Catechism's Approach to the Blessed Virgin Mary", finding it guilty of — horror of horrors — "pre-Vatican II" thinking. She expressed the hope that "during the preparation of local catechisms issues raised by feminist theologians concerning Mariology will be given due consideration".[14]

Fr Neil Brown criticised the Catechism for opting for "a stable and coherent understanding of current Church teaching, rather than showing the historical and cultural factors that must underpin the Church's constant effort to apply its faith creatively to changing circumstances ... The challenges of history and the insights gained from ongoing human experience are notably absent from this view, which, instead, emphasises the universal and permanent features of 'humanity' down through the ages".[15]

So much for the best efforts of the world's bishops and their theological advisers, not to mention the Pope himself.

Since then, the Catechism has become a fact of life for over a decade, becoming the major source book for many new catechetical programs. These days it is no longer so openly criticised; rather in many centres of religious education it is simply ignored, watered down, and given a few token mentions.

Women priests

Further controversy ensued during 1994 with publication of John Paul II's Apostolic Letter, *Ordinatio Sacerdotalis*, which restated that "the Church has no authority whatsoever to confer priestly ordination on women, and that this judgment is to be definitively held by all the faithful". It called for an end to debate or discussion of the subject within the Church, since it was a doctrinal matter that was now closed.[16]

The Pope's letter had become necessary because of the continuing dissent expressed in theological circles. This had intensified following the decision of the Church of England to admit women to the priesthood in 1992.

In Australia, several major Catholic organisations expressed public criticisms or reservations about the content of the Pope's letter.

Members of the National Executive of the Australian Conference of Leaders of Religious Institutes, representing almost 12,000 male and female religious and approximately 170 religious congregations of sisters, priests and brothers, issued a public statement rejecting the Pope's letter. The Australian Conference comprises the leaders of all these congregations, although some religious would later dissociate themselves from this public dissent.[17]

The religious leaders' statement expressed "dismay and disappointment at the recent Apostolic Letter of the Holy Father, Pope John Paul II, specifically in so far as it prohibits further discussion of the ordination of women".

They claimed that the Pope had failed to advance "any arguments other than those espoused in the previous Instructions, *Inter Insigniores* (1976) and *Mulieris Dignitatem* (1988)", yet had "seen fit to embargo any further discussion within the Roman Catholic Church of this very important and evolving issue".

They noted that "the International Biblical Commission reported that there was no conclusive scriptural evidence either supporting or interdicting the ordination of women" and they did not "consider it to be a sufficient response in the present context merely to reassert that this has always been the tradition".

They concluded, "we join with many other Christians in requesting that the question whether women, as well as men, should be admitted to the ranks of the ordained ministry should continue to be considered as a suitable topic for further theological and scriptural research and discussion within the Roman Catholic community".

The Australian Catholic Theological Association at its conference in Melbourne considered the "challenges posed by the Pope's recent letter on the ordination of women". While not directly critical, the Association's statement suggested it did not regard the Pope's letter as the final word on the subject.[18]

The Association decided to set up two committees, one to study "the precise authority of the document and its implications for theology" and the second to "examine the arguments which have been made for and against women's ordination" and "whether they are persuasive and are consistent with the dignity of women".

The Catholic Biblical Association of Australia, during its Annual Meeting on 1-4 July 1994 at Corpus Christi College, Clayton, Victoria, also discussed the Pope's Apostolic Letter.[19]

In its statement, the Association said that "while acknowledging the authority of the Letter, the members of the Association expressed disquiet, as biblical scholars, at the way Scripture is used in this document". The Association recommended that "further studies be undertaken to build on the significant biblical research already available in relation to ministry in the New Testament, especially women's ministry".

Meanwhile, the same Thomas Groome whose methodology has underpinned catechetical programs in a number of Australian dioceses would declare that "the continued exclusion of women from ordained ministry in the Catholic Church is seen by fair-minded scholars as without theological or biblical warrant".[20]

Dissent

In 1998, in order to address the continuing and persistent challenging of Church authority, John Paul issued an Apostolic Letter, *Ad Tuendam Fidem* (To Defend the Faith), which authorised key additions to the *Code of Canon Law*. He explained that these were necessary so as to "defend the faith of the Catholic Church from errors that arise on the part of some faithful".[21]

The Apostolic Letter was distributed by the Vatican press office on 30 June 1998, together with a commentary from Cardinal Ratzinger.

Since 1989, bishops, theologians and others in responsible teaching positions had been required to take an oath of fidelity and make a profession of faith when assuming office. The Pope's document enshrined this requirement in Canon Law, with an additional paragraph to Canon 750 of the Latin code, and Canon 598 of the Eastern code, extending the obligations of Catholics beyond simply believing "all that is contained in the written Word of God and all that has been proclaimed as being divinely revealed".

The new paragraph, underlining the assent required when dealing with Church teachings not proclaimed as divinely revealed, but taught as belonging to the Catholic faith and its unbroken tradition, stated:

"Each and every thing definitively proposed by the magisterium of the Church regarding faith and morals, that is those which are required in order to piously safeguard and faithfully expound the deposit of faith, also must be firmly accepted and held; one who denies the propositions which are to be held definitively, therefore, opposes the doctrine of the Catholic Church".

The second change ordered by the Pope applied Church penalties to those who deny any such "definitive teachings".

The Holy See regarded these changes as necessary because many Catholic theologians had been using the concept of the "hierarchy of truths" to justify dissent against teachings not infallibly defined by the Extraordinary Magisterium. Hence *Ad Tuendam Fidem* stated that the "ordinary magisterium," namely the Church teaching authority exercised by the Pope and the College of Bishops in union with him, also proposed definitive teachings requiring firm acceptance by Catholics.

Thomas Groome's response was that this was "a pretentious attempt by the present Pope to stifle conversation and dialogue", adding, "I read the blessed thing and without being too melodramatic, I was on the verge of tears. It is a very sad day".[22]

Other teachings

Up until the time of his death in 2005, John Paul II continued to write or authorise a succession of documents restating doctrines and disciplines. This had become necessary because so many highly placed Church experts were disputing or undermining them.

In September 2000, a doctrinal statement, *Dominus Jesus*, authorised by the Pope, affirmed the Catholic Church's teaching that it is the "one, true Church of Jesus Christ". It rejected trends, often claiming to be in the "spirit of Vatican II", which involved an exaggerated ecumenism diluting the Church's claims to truth, a religious pluralism equating the beliefs of all world religions and a reluctance among some missioners to seek converts from other faiths.

In regard to the priesthood, John Paul's annual Holy Thursday Letters had provided continuing in-depth instruction since 1979. In his Letter for 2000, he reaffirmed the Church's teachings on the meaning and role of the priesthood and the Eucharist.

However, many priests never saw these inspirational letters, unless they subscribed to *L'Osservatore Romano* or followed the Internet.

In his 2004 Letter, the Pope appealed to parish communities, and priests in particular, to show special care for altar servers who represented a "garden" of priestly vocations. "The group of altar servers", he said, "under your guidance as part of the parish community, can be given a valuable experience of Christian education and become a kind of pre-seminary".[23]

In light of these comments, it is difficult to see where female altar servers, no longer prohibited following a Vatican interpretation of *The Code of Canon Law,* fit into this scheme of things. Clearly John Paul had in mind male altar servers as potential priests. Priests and bishops are under no obligation to allow female altar servers, although they are often pressured to do so.

In October 2002, a Vatican Instruction on the priesthood with the Pope's authorisation was released.[24] It was titled *The Priest, Pastor and Leader of the Parish Community*, and emphasised the "irreplace-

able" sacramental role of the pastor and his need for holiness.

The document focused on the distinction between the roles of the priest and the lay faithful, following closely the line indicated by John Paul II in his Allocution to the Plenary Assembly of the Congregation for Clergy in November 2001. This was included as an introduction.

A priest, it said, "should be a model of adherence to the perennial Magisterium of the Church and to its discipline" with a "profound, genuine and vital bond of communion with the See of Peter" and an "acceptance, diffusion, and conscientious application of papal documents, and of other documents published by the Dicasteries of the Roman Curia".

On Holy Thursday, 17 April 2003, John Paul II released his 14th encyclical, *Ecclesia de Eucharistia*, which contained reminders of important matters raised in earlier papal and Vatican writings, e.g, Sunday Mass obligation, confession, Eucharistic adoration, the real presence, the Mass as a sacrifice, the priesthood, intercommunion, Church music and architecture, and liturgical abuses.[25]

The Pope's strongest language in the encyclical was reserved for the on-going problem of liturgical abuses.[26] "It must be lamented," he said, "that, especially in the years following the post-conciliar liturgical reform, as a result of a misguided sense of creativity and adaptation there have been a number of abuses which have been a source of suffering for many. A certain reaction against 'formalism' has led some, especially in certain regions, to consider the 'forms' chosen by the Church's great liturgical tradition and her Magisterium as non-binding and to introduce unauthorised innovations which are often completely inappropriate".

In order to address the problem, John Paul said that he had asked "the competent offices of the Roman Curia to prepare a more specific document, including prescriptions of a juridical nature, on this very important subject".

The following year the Congregation for Divine Worship and the Discipline of the Sacraments issued the instruction *Redemptionis Sacramentum*, "on certain matters to be observed or to be avoided regarding the Most Holy Eucharist" while upholding the right of lay people to complain about liturgical abuses.[27] Details from this document were cited in Chapter Three.

Legacy

John Paul II worked tirelessly to undo the damage caused by distorted post-Vatican II renewal with his writings and addresses covering every aspect of Church doctrine and discipline under challenge.

But despite his efforts it is doubtful whether one Australian Catholic in a hundred could name any of the Pope's 14 encyclicals, let alone summarise their contents. Despite John Paul's clarification of Catholic teachings in light of Vatican II, many Catholics, if they are interested at all, will be more likely to encounter some local theologian's spin.

Even following his death, amid the warm tributes, including many from people outside the Catholic Church, a sour note was struck by an article in *The Swag*, official journal of the National Council of Priests of Australia, which presented a dismissive assessment of the late pontiff.[28]

The anonymous priest author described the late Pope as a "mixed blessing" because he had failed to listen "to the many voices within and without the Church" and preferred "edicts" to "embraces". John Paul II, the writer claimed, had a "siege" mentality, and "neutralised or dismantled ... most of the momentous spirit of Vatican II". The writer even suggested the Pope was more like "an obstinate European Monarch struggling to hold to his powerful influence" than a so-called "Suffering Servant", as John Paul had come to be called during his final heroic years of physical infirmity.

Other criticisms included John Paul II's alleged ignorance of Scripture scholarship and his "Theology of the Body". According to the writer, "One sad thing about our late Holy Father, while he frequently read Scripture he seemed unaware of the great advances in biblical scholarship that throw new light on sacred texts. Often his preaching was ponderous and his fundamentalist citing of Scripture embarrassing".

The Swag's anonymous commentator continued, "An obsessive interest in what is benignly named 'A Theology of the Body' and the Church looks as preoccupied as ever with sexual matters. From the high moral ground of these utterances, it is [not] hard to see what disruption these noises make for people struggling to make human partnerships work.

"It's just silly to tell educated people that not only are women ineligible for Orders but that it's almost a sin to even think about it. Theological arguments are very thin defending the status quo, and Scripture scholars tell [us] that they find nothing in the New Testament to prevent women being admitted to Orders. The Spirit works through the social sciences and culture too".

Such dissenting views may not have reflected those of *The Swag's* editorial board, but this board did not consider them inappropriate for a journal mailed out to Australia's priests by an organisation claiming to represent them. That in itself reflected poorly on those running the National Council of Priests.

It was a further example of the opposition from many key parts of the Church in Australia to efforts at restoring orthodoxy. It also underlined the obstacles facing any bishops serious about implementing the teachings of John Paul II and his successor.

Endnotes

1. Bishop Kevin Manning, "Making sense of *Veritatis Splendor*", a talk at the Thomas More Centre Summer School, February 1994.
2. *The Australian*, 27 September 1994.
3. *The Canberra Times*, 5 October 1994.
4. *The Australian*, 6 October 1994.
5. *The Australian*, 13 October 1994.
6. B.A. Santamaria, editorial "The Pope: for or against him?", *AD2000*, November 1993, p. 2.
7. Fr James Murray, "ABC *Four Corners* debates the new encyclical", *AD2000*, November 1993, p. 9.
8. Quoted in *AD2000*, April 1990, p. 8.
9. Statement from the US monthly journal, *Commonweal,* referred to in *AD2000*, April 1990, p. 8.
10. The Catholic Institute of Sydney, *The New Catechism: Analysis and Commentary*, 1994.
11. op. cit., p. 12.
12. op. cit., p. 23.
13. op. cit., p. 32, p. 34.
14. op. cit., p. 42.

15. op. cit., p. 79.
16. Apostolic Letter on Reserving Priestly Ordination to Men Alone, *Ordinatio Sacerdotalis*, Pope John Paul II, 22 May 1994.
17. "Religious orders, associations refuse to accept definitive Papal teaching", *AD2000*, p. 3, p. 6.
18. Ibid.
19. Ibid.
20. Thomas Groome, *Language for a Catholic Church*, Revised Edition, Sheed & Ward, 1995, p. 31.
21. "Pope's new Apostolic Letter puts theological dissenters on notice", *AD2000*, AD2000 Report, August 1998, p. 3.
22. Quoted in Eamonn Keane, "Thomas Groome: his influence on religious education continues", *AD2000*, December 2002-January 2003, p. 8.
23. "Overall a boom time for seminaries", *AD2000*, May 2004, p. 4.
24. "New Vatican Instruction on priesthood: the challenge to be another Christ", *AD2000*, December 2002-January 2003, p. 3.
25. *Ecclesia de Eucharistia*, Pope John Paul II, 17 April 2003.
26. op. cit., 52.
27. Congregation for Divine Worship and the Discipline of the Sacraments, Instruction *Redemptionis Sacramentum*, 25 March 2004.
28. *The Swag*, Journal of the National Council of Priests, Spring 2005.

Chapter Eight

Statement of Conclusions

The present condition of the Church in Australia owes much to a false irenicism that has dominated episcopal thinking since the late 1960s. This comfort zone approach, which seeks peace and compromise at the expense of theological truth, has been increasingly challenged by the Holy See, especially since the advent of John Paul II, with bishops repeatedly urged to show greater courage and zeal in teaching the faith.

In *Veritatis Splendor*, John Paul II set out the responsibilities of Church leaders.[1] His words were particularly applicable to Australia. "We have the duty, as Bishops", he said, "to be vigilant that the word of God is faithfully taught. My Brothers in the Episcopate, it is part of our pastoral ministry to see to it that this moral teaching is faithfully handed down and to have recourse to appropriate measures to ensure that the faithful are guarded from every doctrine and theory contrary to it".

He continued, "As Bishops, we have the grave obligation to be personally vigilant that the 'sound doctrine' (1 Tim 1:10) of faith and morals is taught in our Dioceses. A particular responsibility is incumbent upon Bishops with regard to Catholic institutions. Whether these are agencies for the pastoral care of the family or for social work, or institutions dedicated to teaching or health care, Bishops can canonically erect and recognise these structures and delegate certain responsibilities to them. Nevertheless, Bishops are never relieved of their own personal obligations. It falls to them, in communion with the Holy See, both to grant the title 'Catholic' to Church-related schools, universities, health-care facilities and counselling services, and, in cases of a serious failure to live up to that title, to take it away".

But while some church bodies in Australia arguably no longer warrant the label Catholic, few if any bishops appear prepared to grasp the nettle.

Ad Limina

The continuing evidence of declining beliefs and practices no doubt prompted a dramatic calling to account of the Australian hierarchy during its ad limina visit to Rome in late 1998.

Ad limina visits are undertaken every five years at which times the bishops report on developments in their dioceses and receive guidance, where necessary, on how better to administer the local Church.

Never in Australia's history, however, was the guidance to be as wide-ranging, specific and urgently expressed as on this visit.

The Pope met the bishops at the end of their visit, which also included attendance at the Synod of the Bishops of Oceania and consultations between 15 bishops representing the Australian Episcopal Conference and 12 prefects and secretaries of six dicasteries of the Roman Curia — including the Congregations for Bishops and for the Doctrine of the Faith — on the state of the Catholic Church in Australia.

These consultations culminated in a summary document called *Statement of Conclusions* which was signed by the Australian and Curial representatives. Prominent among the latter was Cardinal Joseph Ratzinger, the future Pope Benedict XVI. His knowledge of the state of the Church in Australia as Prefect of the Congregation of the Doctrine of the Faith for over 20 years would be unrivalled.

John Paul II, commenting later on the Statement in his concluding message to the Australian bishops before they headed back to their dioceses, said, "I earnestly recommend to your prayer and reflection, to your responsibility and action, the document which summarises your meetings with the various Dicasteries of the Holy See". He then lent emphasis to many of the document's key recommendations.[2]

"Your meetings with some of the Congregations of the Roman

Curia have focused on questions of doctrine and morality, the liturgy, the role of the Bishop, evangelisation and mission, the priesthood, religious life, and Catholic education. In each of these areas, your own personal responsibility is vital ... Each individual bishop, then, is called to assume his full responsibility, setting his face resolutely against all that might harm the faith that has been handed down (cf I Cor 4:7)".

The *Statement of Conclusions* itself acknowledged positive aspects of the Church in Australia, including the increasing proportion of Catholics in the population. But then followed a catalogue of problems needing urgent episcopal attention, encompassing the major areas of Church life.

John Paul II then rather tellingly noted in his address, "Until recently, the Catholic community in Australia knew nothing but consistent growth ... Now perhaps it appears that the momentum has slackened". With, in some dioceses, weekly Mass attendances down to less than ten percent and vocations to the priesthood almost non-existent, that was putting it very kindly.

The Statement offered a number of general observations about

Some of the Australian bishops in St Peter's during the Synod of Oceania in 1998

what it called the "crisis in faith" in Australia that reflected the influence of secularism. The crisis encompassed a declining belief in God, an afterlife and the inspiration of the Scriptures, with Christ reduced in many cases to just "a great prophet of humanity" and the Church to a body of purely human origin. Truth for many was now based on "the shifting sands of majority and consensus".[3]

A bishop's responsibility

Central to any progress in addressing this crisis of faith was the responsibility of each bishop to "affirm, admonish and correct according to what the specific circumstances require". The clear implication was that some Australian bishops were failing to do this. "The People of God," said the Statement, "look to their shepherds for guidance and leadership now more than ever in these confusing and increasingly secularised times". Each bishop was called to exercise "the three-fold office of teaching, sanctifying and governing".[4]

The teaching of the bishops had to be "in union with the Holy Father and the Magisterium of the Church" while "the People of God who are entrusted to their care have a right to receive authentic and clear Catholic teaching from those who represent the Church in its various institutions".

The document continued: "It is their grave responsibility, clearly and unambiguously, to proclaim the Church's teaching and to do all that they can to preserve the faithful from error ... The bishop may not tolerate error in matters of doctrine and morals or Church discipline, and true unity must never be at the expense of truth".

In his office of sanctifying, the Statement emphasised, a bishop should "exercise vigilance over the celebration and administration of the sacraments in his diocese" ensuring these "are administered according to the proper liturgical norms ... If he discovers that these norms are not being followed properly, with integrity and reverence, he acts quickly to correct the error or abuse ... The Australian bishops realise that the sacred Liturgy is at the heart of their pastoral responsibilities".

As for the third area, governing, in "choosing their collaborators in the diocesan administration, seminary and in parishes, bishops need to make these appointments with a careful eye and with great attention, always giving emphasis to sanctity of life, orthodoxy and pastoral competence. Continual vigilance is imperative in order to safeguard the integrity of the Faith and to ensure that it is clearly taught and explained at all levels of diocesan life".

Priesthood

The Statement then examined specific areas of the Church's life that had been under challenge in recent decades.

In the case of the priesthood, a priest's identity needed "strong affirmation and almost constant clarification". In order to "ensure this understanding it is fundamental that correct intellectual, ascetical and doctrinal formation, as well as dutiful and inspired discipline, be assured in seminaries".[5]

Seminary education needed to be "characterised by a clear and authentic idea of the ministerial priesthood, its specificity and its relationship to the priesthood of all the baptised". This "should be based on a sound Christology and ecclesiology, as transmitted by the Church" with these understandings "clear in the minds of both the teachers and the students". A conviction about the "relationship of celibacy to their priestly vocation" should be nourished among seminarians along with a commitment to its observance.

Priests in difficult pastoral situations ought not compromise the faith. "No pastoral solution can be so-called", it said, "that is not flowing from God's Revelation as this is interpreted by the Magisterium of the Church. Thus a practice in pastoral life, which is contrary to the teachings of Christ and His Church, is not an act of compassion, but rather one that radically disorders pastoral charity and has long term negative consequences for the faithful".

In a significant move, and one directed at problems in some Catholic education offices and schools, the document declared that "the matter of catechesis cannot be left solely in the hands of others, no matter how skilled they be. The transmission of the Faith is to be actively attended to by priests as this is an essential part of their ministry [in the course of which they should refer to the new *Catechism*]".

Religious life

Next the state of religious life was examined, with reference made to defective formation.[6] Problems arose here "because the selection of formators or of centres of ongoing formation was not made in view of full communion with the Magisterium of the Church". The widespread practice among the larger established religious orders of having their members live in flats and private houses was criticised as fragmenting "the life and witness of an Institute" and prejudicing "the corporate witness of an Institute which was founded with a specific charism for a specific purpose". It urged a restoration of community life.

However, while the more traditional and more recently founded religious orders continue to have a strong community life, many of the larger orders that formerly taught in Catholic schools continue to fragment and lose their identity.

Public dissent on the part of prominent male and female religious was noted. "Consecrated persons," said the Statement, "are called to be mindful of the ancient dictum: *sentire cum ecclesia*, to live and think and love with the Church. In this regard, *Vita Consecrata* [the Vatican document on religious life] is very explicit. A distinctive aspect of ecclesial communion is allegiance of mind and heart to the Magisterium of the bishops, an allegiance which must be lived honestly and clearly testified to before the People of God by all consecrated persons, especially those involved in theological research, teaching, publishing, catechesis and the use of the means of social communication".

The prominent place religious enjoyed within the Catholic community placed a particular onus on these religious to demonstrate "a more evident fidelity to the Magisterium than is required of ordinary faithful". Following publicly dissenting statements from some leaders of religious orders in recent years, the Statement insisted, "What is true of all religious is even more true of major superiors, by reason of their office. What is true of major superiors is still more true of a conference of major superiors erected by the Holy See".

The divided state of the Church is especially evident among Australia's religious orders, with orthodox communities and individual members of larger orders preferring to belong to the Association for the Promotion of Religious Life, an organisation fully committed to the Church's Magisterium. At the same time, some members of the larger religious orders, now living on borrowed time, have gravitated into the New Age (see Chapter 2) and political activism as a result of creative interpretations of their orders' charisms (reasons for foundation in the first place).

Significantly, it is the orthodox religious orders, with their commitment to community life, such as the Missionaries of Charity, that continue to attract vocations. Those orders that have lost their identity, or become politicised or secularised, are living on borrowed time.

Liturgy

Regarding liturgy[7], the *Statement of Conclusions* called for "a special reverence for the Real Presence of Christ in the Holy Eucharist at the Mass and reserved in the tabernacle" and called on Australia's bishops to confront the reality of liturgical abuses. "In today's rapidly changing world," it said, "it is all the more necessary to return constantly to the authentic teaching of the Church on the Liturgy, as found in the liturgical texts themselves ... The tendency on the part of some priests and parishes to make their own changes to liturgical texts and structures, whether by omissions, by additions, or by substitutions, occasionally even in central texts such as the Eucharistic Prayer" had to be stopped.

The Statement continued, "Practices foreign to the Roman Rite are not to be introduced on the private initiative of priests, who are ministers and servants, rather than masters of the sacred rites ... The bishops of Australia, then, will continue to put their energy above all into education, while correcting these abuses individually".

The Sacrament of Penance was of particular concern. "Energetic efforts," said the Statement, "are to be made to avoid any risk that this traditional practice of the Sacrament of Penance [individual confession] fall into disuse ... Unfortunately, communal celebrations have not infrequently occasioned an illegitimate use of general absolution. This illegitimate use, like other abuses in the administration of the Sacrament of Penance, is to be eliminated".

The growing frequency of illicit general absolutions was symptomatic of the overall dumbing down of the faith including the virtual disappearance of fasting and abstinence, holy days of obligation, mention of Hell and mortal sin, and anything else that might be too "difficult" for modern Catholics. Regular confession, along with belief in Christ's real presence in the Eucharist, has always been a reliable litmus test of commitment to the Catholic faith. From these flow the good works that are part and parcel of being a practising Christian.

In many parishes, it is now almost impossible to have one's confession heard without prior appointment — a major disincentive for Catholics who prefer anonymity.

Bishops' Letter

In April 1999, the Australian Catholic Bishops Conference took place at Kensington, Sydney, to consider the contents of the *Statement of Conclusions*.

For the first time since Vatican II, after years of denial, the Church's leadership in Australia had been obliged collectively to acknowledge a deepening crisis of faith along with the need for remedial action. At the end of their conference, the bishops issued a document titled *Letter from the Australian Bishops to the Catholic People of Australia*.[9]

The Bishops' Letter noted John Paul II's strong endorsement of the *Statement of Conclusions* and his insistence that the bishops take action to address key problem areas. "The Pope," it said, "reminds bishops that they 'may not tolerate error in matters of doctrine and morals or Church discipline'."

The Bishops' Letter pinpointed the crux of the matter:[10] "By most measurable criteria such as religious affiliation, church attendance, vocations, marriage in church, etc, secularisation is making great inroads in Australia. This indicates a crisis of faith. Within the Church there are different understandings of the person of Jesus Christ, the nature of the Church, the role of conscience and various moral problems, and not all understandings are in agreement with Catholic teaching. Some less than appropriate practices can at times take place at liturgical celebrations".

The Letter then indicated the bishops would be following the Pope's request that the use of the Third Rite of reconciliation (general absolution) "be kept strictly within the conditions laid down by Canon Law". Under Australian conditions, that basically meant not to be celebrated at all.[11]

Prior to the Bishops Conference, in an apparent response to the reluctance of several Australian bishops, including Archbishop Leonard Faulkner of Adelaide, to clamp down on illicit Third Rite celebrations, the Vatican Congregation for Divine Worship and Discipline of the Sacraments issued a three-page document (dated 19 March 1999) emphatically re-stating the Church's teaching on the Sacrament of Penance.[12]

The document drew attention to the situation in Australia, which had caused concern in Rome. "In recent years", it said, "in spite of repeated clarifications given by the Holy See on the necessary conditions for the valid and licit administration of the Sacrament of Penance, there has been an increasing demand for the indiscriminate use of 'general absolution'."

The Congregation indicated that its document was designed to remove "any remaining doubt or confusion regarding this matter" and to make clear the existing "law in force" on "the essential conditions for the ordinary and extraordinary celebration of the sacrament in the Latin Church".

Opposition

Despite the direct language, and the joint agreement of the Australian bishops to keep general absolutions strictly under control, several bishops seemed to be having second thoughts with Bishop Heenan of Rockhampton indicating he would leave it to his priests to decide on use of the Third Rite, while the practice would persist in the Diocese of Toowoomba, Queensland, and in individual parishes elsewhere.

The Holy See's hardline approach was greeted with dismay by Archbishop Bathersby of Brisbane, who said he was "hurt, bothered, distressed and above all angry", asking himself, "How could the Pope have so badly misjudged the Australian Church?"

He then launched into a general criticism of the *Statement of Conclusions*. He said he knew the Church in Australia "wasn't perfect" but he "didn't think that it needed the rather sharp criticism that seemed to be present in the document". He was disappointed that "the great strength of the Australian Church, its pastoral intimacy", seemed to be "called into question".[13]

Apart from some unhappy bishops, the condition of whose dioceses seems to have prompted the *Statement of Conclusions* in the first place, the Church's liberals were clearly dismayed at the turn of events and were soon organising opposition.

A joint three-day conference of the National Council of Priests and the Leaders of Religious Institutes, held in Sydney in February 1999 to discuss the *Statement of Conclusions*, issued their own statement which strongly disputed the document.[14] It rejected the call for a curb on general absolution, and criticised the Statement's failure to address the question of clerical celibacy. It complained that the Vatican's "overwhelmingly negative estimation" of Australian Catholicism did not reflect their own "broad experience of the Church here". The National Council of Priests' chairman, Father Gary Russell of Brisbane, alleged that the Vatican had been given the wrong impression by "extremist" members of the Church — "extremist" being liberal code for orthodox Catholics.

Taking this a stage further, Catalyst for Renewal, a recently formed body comprising some of the Church's more prominent liberals, organised a "Public Forum on the *Statement of Conclusions*" in the Sydney Town Hall on 22 April.

Prior to the Forum, Catalyst's Executive Director, Fr Michael Whelan SM, described the criticisms of Australian Catholicism contained in the *Statement of Conclusions* as "offensive" and lacking in an understanding of the "Australian Church". It was based, he said, on "negative material" sent to the "Roman Curia by sources other than the bishops who actually met with them". This in turn was being used to force "our bishops to knuckle under".[15]

This is the familiar liberal litany, that Rome swallows whatever is sent by "right-wingers" and "arch-conservatives". These people, in truth, have been sending documentations of abuses to local bishops for years with little if any result. Appealing to the Holy See has become a last resort, and anyone aware of how slowly the wheels turn there would realise that only watertight, well documented evidence has the slightest hope of drawing any response.

But the obtaining of such evidence is often denounced by the perpetrators and their supporters as "spying" — or that unforgiveable Australian crime of "dobbing in".

The Public Forum's panel of speakers, introduced by the ABC's Geraldine Doogue, comprised Bishop Heenan of Rockhampton, Bishop Geoffrey Robinson, a Sydney auxiliary bishop, Sr Annette Cunliffe RSC, President of the Conference of Leaders of Religious Institutes, Mr Robert Fitzgerald, Community Services Commissioner of New South Wales and Fr Michael Whelan.[16]

Opening the evening's proceedings, Geraldine Doogue said, "Let us listen tonight to the movement of the Holy Spirit in our midst" — although one suspected it was some other kind of spirit, perhaps "the spirit of Vatican II".

Bishop Heenan said he was there because he "loved the Church" and was "concerned by the confusion, the hurt and the division affecting our Church at the present time". He added that the *Statement of Conclusions* was met with "strong disappointment by some of the Australian bishops", many of whom had no input into the final draft which "omitted many of the strengths of the Church" — no doubt including those in his own Diocese of Rockhampton.

Sr Cunliffe said her reaction to the Statement was one of disappointment. It suffered from "internal contradictions" and made no mention of "sexual problems". She referred to the Statement as "an inward looking document" which by its "reference to a decline in the sense of sin" left her "puzzled". The Statement's references to priestly and religious life, she suggested, could contradict Vatican II. It was, she added, "overly simplistic to call for prayer for vocations".

Mr Fitzgerald questioned the Statement's assertion that there was a crisis of faith in the Catholic Church and suggested the real crisis was one of "the institutionalisation of our faith". He elicited enthusiastic applause and laughter from the audience when he said, "We don't shoot those who disagree with the Church in Sydney, though I am not so sure in Melbourne" — a clear reference to Dr George Pell, then Archbishop of Melbourne, and his recent ban on a dissenting book by Fr Michael Morwood.

He pointed to "a crisis of confidence with the Church's ability to deal with the questioning going on", and he declared that with documents like the Statement the Church's leadership "distances itself from the people of the Church". It was "based more on fear of losing what is" and as such "the sign of hope is diminished because of its opposition with authority".

Fr Whelan claimed the process by which the Statement was produced was "manipulated by the Roman Curia" which he believed was seeking to bring about a "centralisation of authority" which "Vatican II wanted to curtail". According to Fr Whelan, the Statement "ignores the vision of the Council and reverts to a rigid vision of Church". The Church, he added, needed to address "the shortcomings of our traditional moral thinking and the hurt it has caused". He concluded with the words, "I must express my loyal opposition".

The final speaker, Bishop Robinson, said he wondered why anyone could doubt the loyalty of the Australian bishops to the Holy Father: "When he [the Pope] asked for an end to the Third Rite, the bishops said 'Yes'." Bishop Robinson said he had no time to go around "dobbing in priests for faults in liturgy".

During question time, Mr Fitzgerald opined, "It is time for the Church to listen to the people who want forgiveness of sins in a new way" and he added that "the will of the people will eventually win out on the question of the Third Rite". Fr Whelan was asked whether the "Second Reformation" had begun, to which he answered, "It is too early to say".

Bishop Heenan, who was one of the group of Australian bishops that met with members of the Vatican Curia to discuss the Church's problems, had meanwhile contributed an article to *The Mix*, Catalyst for Renewal's journal, titled "Why did I sign?"[17]

He provided an answer to this by offering an interesting interpretation of the *Statement of Conclusions*.

"The document speaks in general terms", he said, "avoiding the mention of specific persons, groups, institutions or publications that might be considered problematic. Rather it *provides guidance* to the local bishop to affirm, admonish or correct *as he sees fit* and according to what is called for in each circumstance" (Bishop Heenan's emphases). That meant, in effect, that he need do nothing if there were no problems in his diocese — according to his definition of problems.

However, he was still less than happy with the document for not presenting "the overall picture of the strength of the Australian Church". It had, he said, "sections that show lack of appreciation of the Local

Church living out the Gospel in our culture" and did not "reflect sufficiently the positive contribution the Australian bishops made to the dialogue". By his interpretation, anyone could have signed the document without qualms.

If Bishop Heenan's understanding of the Statement was typical of other bishops, it is no wonder so little has been done since 1999 to implement its unambiguous directives.

Support

By contrast, Bishop Manning of Parramatta defended the Statement in his diocesan paper.[18] "Since returning from Rome", he observed, "I have heard people challenge the Statement's claim that there is a crisis of faith in Australia and that the Roman Curia has misread the situation".

On the contrary, the *Statement of Conclusions* had "the approval of the Australian Bishops" and belonged "as much to them, as it does to members of the Roman Curia". The Australian bishops, he continued, "having signed it are now doing their best to respond to, and help the discussion about it".

Referring to the *Letter from the Australian Bishops*, Bishop Manning said this looked "frankly at the problems that have surfaced" and indicated that he had "met with priests of the diocese and with the religious to discuss the document".

Several dioceses published full texts of the Statement in their newspapers, including Perth, Melbourne and Parramatta. It was clear at least some bishops wanted their people to be fully informed of the situation as a preliminary to implementing the agreed program.

At this point, some long overdue episcopal action might have been anticipated. However, the opportunity passed. Since then the decline in belief and practice has continued, along with evidence of further dissent, despite the clearly formulated agenda the bishops have for tackling problem areas.

Papal and Vatican documents aimed at the crisis have been published over this period, but the gulf keeps widening between their messages and what most Australian Catholics actually know, believe or practise.

Endnotes

1. *Veritatis Splendor*, Encyclical Letter, Pope John Paul II, 6 August 1993, 116.
2. Address of John Paul II to members of the Australian Conference of Bishops during their ad limina apostolorum visit, 14 December 1998, Zenit News Agency.
3. *Statement of Conclusions*, Final Declaration of the Interdicasterial Meeting with a representation of the Australian Bishops and the Roman Curia, 4.
4. op. cit., 10-17.
5. op. cit., 18-24, 48-54.
6. op. cit., 25-36.
7. op. cit., 37-46.
8. op. cit., 55-63.
9. *Letter from the Australian Bishops to the Catholic People of Australia*, Australian Catholic Bishops Conference, 6-15 April 1999.
10. op. cit., par 9.
11. op. cit., par 12.
12. "Bishops Conference resolves crisis over the *Statement of Conclusions*", *AD2000*, June 1999, pp. 3-4.
13. *The Courier-Mail*, 19 February 1999.
14. Joint three-day conference of National Council of Priests and the Leaders of Religious Institutes, Joint Statement, February 1999.
15. *The Catholic Weekly*, 11 April 1999, p. 3.
16. Report on Public Forum at the Sydney Town Hall on 22 April 1999 to discuss the *Statement of Conclusions* by Eamonn Keane and Robert Denahy who both attended the Forum.
17. Bishop Brian Heenan, "Why did I sign?", *The Mix*, Journal of Catalyst for Renewal Incorporated, April 1999, p. 4.
18. *Catholic Outlook* (Parramatta), May 1999.

Chapter Nine

New Leaders

Following Vatican II, there were many breaks with a past seen increasingly as outmoded. This process gained impetus in the late 1960s with the onset of the secular cultural revolution which challenged all forms of authority and tradition.

One area many thought needed a radical overhaul was episcopal leadership. Pre-Vatican II bishops were now seen — with occasional justification — to have been too narrow, inflexible, clericalist and authoritarian.

The post-Conciliar Church, it was thought, called for a different style of leader, one who was more tolerant, inclusive, open to new ideas, democratic in outlook, slow to censor. Bishops with these and other desirable qualities were called "pastoral".

This pattern was evident across the Western world as Apostolic Nuncios and their advisers sought out "pastoral" qualities in potential bishops.

This was already occurring in religious orders and seminaries where new style leaders were dismantling old ways of prayer, worship, community life, attire, discipline, formation and education.

By the 1970s, even with the growing post-Vatican II chaos in evidence, the predominant pastoral style was to stand back and let a hundred flowers bloom.

Dissenting or radical opinions on doctrines, morals and Scripture were given free rein at official Catholic venues, bizarre liturgical practices tolerated, doctrine-less catechetics prescribed with doctrinal catechesis proscribed, and open-ended renewal programs were promoted. Those who questioned the free-for-all were dismissed as "pre-Vatican II" relics in need of re-education or grief counselling.

John Paul II

By the time of John Paul II's election it was obvious, even to some earlier enthusiasts, that things were getting out of hand with a major spiritual disaster looming — certainly in Western nations.

The obvious solution was to appoint bishops more attuned to the current needs of the Church, better able to sift wheat from chaff. This would take time, as many of the pastoral style bishops were relatively young when appointed and still had years to go before retirement. The damage could not be undone overnight.

By the end of John Paul II's long pontificate, most of Australia's large metropolitan dioceses would be led by bishops more cognisant of the state of the Church and what was required to turn things around. However, with smaller dioceses the situation has varied considerably.

But even the stronger John Paul II — and now Benedict XVI — bishops faced an uphill task of repairing the damage after thirty years of misgovernment and general confusion. Reliable human resources were often in short supply, while existing bureaucracies and local minders could prove obstacles.

However, where bishops persevered, choosing dependable advisers and setting up new positions and structures to circumvent the old, there has been some modest progress which is acknowledged in the following case studies.

The two most visible of the new style leaders have been Archbishop Barry Hickey of Perth and Archbishop George Pell of Melbourne — later Cardinal Archbishop of Sydney. The following are a few of their many initiatives to rebuild and enrich their dioceses.

The past decade has seen several other Australian bishops follow a similar path.

Archbishop Hickey

Archbishop Hickey was the first of the new style leaders to take over a large archdiocese when he succeeded the liberal Archbishop William Foley in 1991.

That Archbishop Hickey was well aware of the Church's crisis situation was evident in his appraisal that "from a human point of view we have to admit that if we simply continue to do what we are doing we will get the same outcome. The drift away from the Church will continue. We must therefore look closely at what we are doing and see what still needs to be done".[1]

Despite the difficulties, in the years since taking office, Archbishop Hickey has made some progress against the odds.

He issued a pastoral letter to acknowledge the 25th anniversary of *Humanae Vitae* and celebrated a commemorative Mass in St Mary's Cathedral on Sunday 25 July 1993.[2]

"Today, more so than twenty-five years ago," he said, "the Western world better understands and respects the workings of nature and is more aware of the long-term and harmful effects of foreign substances on the human body ... I wish to reaffirm in this Letter the Church's teaching on contraception lest anyone believe it has been quietly set aside or that it is about to be reversed ... I ask our priests and teachers at every level in the Church to present the full vision of Christian marriage in their preaching and teaching".

In 1996, at the behest of the Archbishop, Pregnancy Assistance Inc was established in Perth, with an office and counselling rooms provided by the Archdiocese. It was the first initiative of its kind in Australia, with Archbishop Hickey its patron.[3] Something similar would later be set up in Sydney by Cardinal Pell.

Since then, its trained counsellors have provided support to women contemplating abortion, saving the lives of many unborn children. Financial assistance has been given where needed and tons of baby clothing and furniture have been gathered and dispensed to families and single mothers in need.

During the centre's first year volunteers provided furnishings for a chapel on the premises where the Blessed Sacrament is reserved and Mass is celebrated three times a week.

In 1999, Bishop Peter Quinn of the neighbouring Western Australian Diocese of Bunbury established a similar agency using the same name.

In 2003, Archbishop Hickey issued a *Pastoral Letter on Chris-*

Archbishop Barry Hickey of Perth

tian Marriage to coincide with World Marriage Day on 9 February.[4] "This day," he said, "is an opportunity to reaffirm the good news of Christian marriage against a background of widespread marriage breakdown and cynicism about marriage itself. What the Church teaches about marriage it does with the full authority of Christ himself ... Let young people heed the Church's call to be chaste before marriage and be faithful within marriage. Experimentation and promiscuity before marriage is not only seriously sinful, it is the worst possible preparation for fidelity within marriage".

In regard to liturgy, Archbishop Hickey did not wait for the *Statement of Conclusions* to provide clear direction. In March 1995, he circulated his priests with a paper titled "Priests and the Eucharistic Liturgy", which instructed, among other things, that:[5]

• A priest should not allow his "personality and skills" to prevail over "the sacred mysteries being celebrated" for "the Mass is never simply the action of the people. It is primarily the action of Christ united with His people".

• Whatever licit "cultural adaptations" reflecting "ethnic traditions, local customs and events" are introduced, "the essential elements of the Mass must always remain intact".

• "Excesses are to be avoided lest the frame become more important than the picture. The essence of the Mass is not to be lost in a host of distractions".

• Priests should use the homily on Sundays and Holy Days to provide not merely Scripture reflections but "a systematic presentation of the Faith" and "should make every effort to link Scripture reflections with daily life and with Church teachings".

• Priests should show proper reverence towards the Blessed Sacrament by means of genuflection, and not by a bow, unless age or infirmity requires it.

• Eucharistic adoration should be encouraged.

In 2003, the Archbishop saw the need to reinforce these instructions. In his regular letter to all priests he requested them to follow the official instructions for the Mass as laid down in the *General Instruction on the Roman Missal*.[6]

Many people, he noted, "rightly complained that some priests disregarded these provisions". His letter instructed:

"For the good of the faithful, and for good order and the dignity of the celebration, I ask all priests to follow what is officially laid down.

"We are not free to make arbitrary changes simply because we think they are better than what has been mandated.

"Certain freedoms and options are already indicated in the *General Instruction*. We may use these but should not introduce idiosyncratic changes".

Regarding evangelisation, the Archbishop backed a lay initiated radio talk-back program, titled "The Layman's Hour", which was launched on 4 February 2001.[7] Its host, Raymond de Souza, was the founder and director of St Gabriel Communications, which specialised in promoting Catholic apologetics. Mr de Souza has travelled widely in Australia and overseas giving talks on the faith.

During a Mass at Mater Dei College in Edgewater, Perth, on 4 February 2004, Archbishop Hickey and auxiliary Bishop Donald Sproxton continued their program of introducing students in Catholic schools to the words of Pope John Paul II.[8]

This was the first presentation for 2004 to Year 12 students of the book *Pope John Paul II Speaks to Youth*, published by Archbishop Hickey and exclusive to students in the Perth Archdiocese. The book consisted of the essence of the Pope's many addresses to young people around the world, grouped under headings such as vocation, freedom, love, peace and service.

In other areas since 1991, Archbishop Hickey has given regular brief talks on prime time Perth television on moral and ethical issues, and reactivated the Perth seminary of St Charles, bringing back Western Australia's seminarians from the liberal Adelaide seminary, which subsequently closed down due to a lack of numbers. Under his leadership, the number of seminarians has increased significantly over the past decade. (More details in next chapter).

In addition, the archdiocesan weekly, *The Record*, has become the best of its kind in Australia, with comprehensive international news coverage and strongly Catholic content, thanks to the editorship of David Kehoe and his successor Peter Rosengren. Mr Rosengren also edits *Discovery*, an excellent bi-monthly "Catholic magazine for families".

Late in 2005, Archbishop Hickey signalled that he was pushing for a substantial improvement in the quality of RE teaching in the Archdiocese. He told his priests that sustained efforts would be made to find suitable teachers who would teach RE on a full-time basis.

"They are not easy to find", he said, "but there are already some in our schools and their numbers are growing ... This is a very good option to pursue because, while not all teachers want to teach RE, others see it as the main reason why they are teaching in Catholic schools".[9]

Cardinal Pell

Cardinal George Pell, Archbishop of Sydney, already the subject of a biography and well known internationally, has been, for close on twenty years, Australia's highest profile bishop.

His reputation as a defender of Church teachings in the secular media was well developed from the time he was appointed an auxiliary bishop in Melbourne in 1987. He has served on Vatican congregations and been an outspoken supporter and defender of John Paul II's leadership and teachings.

In 1988, when many Australian bishops were still in denial about the worsening crisis of faith, Bishop Pell offered a healthy dose of realism.[10]

"The worldwide Catholic community," he said, "has gone through a period of religiously-inspired change since the Second Vatican Council (1962-1965), greater than any changes since the Protestant Reformation in the 16th century. Such changes were introduced here without hesitation by local bishops, who were strong exponents of Roman obedience and blissfully ignorant, at least initially, of the sociological consequences of the revolution they were effecting".

Bishop Pell even contemplated the possibility of a remnant situation. "It is theoretically possible," he suggested, "that defence of the core traditions might mean a smaller Church". Despite this, he said, "we should still stick with the tradition". In any case, he continued, "we shall slow the exodus from the Church and attract more converts not only by defending and developing the core of Catholicism, but also by energetically promoting many aspects of the style of Australian Catholicism, which we have been tempted to down play for reasons of ecumenism or as concessions to modernity".

There should be no watering down of the faith. "Children in our Catholic schools," he insisted, "should be told regularly that Catholics should attend Sunday Mass and that the Ten Commandments are part

Cardinal George Pell

of Divine Revelation", while "the doctrine of the primacy of conscience should be quietly ditched, at least in our schools, or comprehensively restated, because too many Catholic youngsters have concluded that values are personal inventions, that we can paint our moral pictures any way we choose".

Such sentiments would not have endeared Dr Pell to Melbourne's well-entrenched "spirit of Vatican II" elites nor, perhaps, would these elites have welcomed the announcement of his appointment in 1996 as the new Archbishop of Melbourne, to succeed Archbishop Frank Little who had led the archdiocese since 1974.

Archbishop Pell's impact was not long in coming. In late 1996, he persuaded Victoria's other bishops and the Archbishop of Hobart (Tasmania) to accept a set of modest reforms to the languishing Corpus Christi Seminary, which trained future priests for Victoria's four dioceses as well as the state of Tasmania. The faculty took these reforms as an adverse reflection on their running of the seminary and submitted their resignations — which Archbishop Pell promptly accepted. He then appointed a new staff more attuned to the needs of priestly formation. (More details on this are in the next chapter).

Since then seminary numbers have risen significantly from their 1996 low point, and continued to do so under Archbishop Pell's successor since 2001, Archbishop Denis Hart.

In 1998, in another important move, Archbishop Pell took steps to address the inadequacies of the current religion curriculum in the Melbourne Archdiocese.

Since the 1970s, a set of Guidelines produced by the Catholic Education Office had followed a student-centred approach, mimicking trends in secular education, that was shallow and often deficient doctrinally.

One of the Archbishop's first key appointments was of Monsignor Peter Elliott, who had worked for many years in Rome in the Pontifical Council for the Family. Msgr Elliott was made Episcopal Vicar for Religious Education, with executive oversight for all Catholic religious education in the schools, parishes and catechetical centres of the Archdiocese. This position was separate from the Catholic Education Office.

The first task entrusted to him was supervision of the preparation, writing and editing of religious education texts for all levels in Catholic schools. This project would take several years to complete and at the secondary level the degree of school and teacher co-operation varied.

The series of texts called *To Know, Worship and Love* would, in line with John Paul II's *Catechesi Tradendae*, place a strong emphasis on the cognitive dimension of religious education. "In practical terms," said Msgr Elliott, "we should give children more credit for a capacity to absorb concepts" since "Even the smallest children are able to grasp and memorise key doctrines".[11]

The texts presented core Church teachings and prayers to be memorised in line with the new *Directory for Catechesis* published in 1997 by the Congregation for the Clergy in Rome, with their content derived from the *Catechism of the Catholic Church*.

The architects of failure were soon on the offensive, courtesy of the liberal *Sunday Age* which used copies of the draft text books as the basis for a large feature headlined, "The Pell Papers: The Revolution in Catholic Classrooms".[12] It would be part of that newspaper's ongoing campaign against Archbishop Pell's leadership, with generous page space made available to the Church's dissenters.

Martin Daly, religion writer for *The Sunday Age*, wrote, "Critics argue that the drafts — obtained by *The Sunday Age* — appear designed to force primary and secondary students at more than 300 schools into a male-oriented Catholicism that is out of touch with the realities of the modern church and gives the impression that Christians other than Catholics are second-class citizens".

With unconscious irony, Daly quoted "the critics" suggesting that a return to religion texts could "potentially" ensure "many young people will not embrace the Catholic faith or that they will do so in a state of confusion and doubt". In fact, the critics here were describing the very situation their favoured approach had contributed to over the preceding 30 years.

Among the critics, Fr Paul Collins said the Melbourne project conveyed "the feeling that if Pope John XXIII called for the windows in the church to be opened, this approach to religious education is determined to close them again".

Fr Michael Morwood said the texts had a "narrow, insular, seriously flawed view of the beginnings of human history" because they followed "the doctrinal framework of the *Catechism of the Catholic Church*" and its "literalist interpretation" of original sin and Jesus as redeemer: "'By his sacrifice on the cross, Jesus became our Redeemer'.

This is terrible stuff ... It's a very narrow interpretation of Jesus' role as redeemer and conjures up ideas of a sacrificial death to appease God".

Dr Robert Crotty, Professor of Religious Education at the University of South Australia, called for the whole project to be scrapped. "The Church", he declared, "has struggled to invigorate its ritual, its liturgy. It is still trying to teach the young how to act out their religion. The project will reverse the trend. It is a return to the mechanism of the past sub-group, which had to identify who was in and who was out by employing strange prayers and practices. What to do with this project? Scrap it. Could religious educators please stand up and refuse to endorse it. Its implementation would mean the loss of a generation of real faith and real religious community".

With such mind-sets still embedded in Australia's religious education establishments, as well as in the thousands of Catholic teachers trained since the late 1960s, it was clear that implementation of any reformed approach faced major hurdles.

Archbishop Pell caused further outrage among liberal Catholics and their media allies during 1998 when he withheld Communion from activists wearing rainbow sashes to signal their opposition to Church teaching on homosexual acts.

In response, the Archbishop issued a public statement explaining the Church's position. "While I accept", he said, "that people may hold views on the proper expression of their sexual life and identity which differ from the Church's teachings, I deeply regret that such people — who profess the Catholic faith — would choose to mount an ideological demonstration during Mass and especially at Communion time".

He continued, "We have had these protests before. Probably they will be with us for quite a time yet. I will pray for the protesters. But they must realise that the Church's teaching on this matter cannot, will not, change".[13]

Later in 1998, in a pastoral letter, titled "On Life and Love," to mark the 30th anniversary of Pope Paul VI's encyclical *Humanae Vitae*, Archbishop Pell re-stated the Catholic Church's continuing opposition to contraception and called for society to take stock of the costs of the sexual revolution made possible by the pill.

The pastoral letter was issued to all parishes and all Year 11 and 12 students in Catholic secondary schools in the Melbourne Archdiocese.[14]

The pastoral letter would prompt further public anger — via the secular media — from the Church's liberals.

In 1998, Archbishop Pell took firm action against a widely used reference book on the Catholic faith by Fr Michael Morwood, titled *Tomorrow's Catholic: Understanding God and Jesus in a New Millennium*. The Archbishop's "Notice" regarding Morwood's book stated that it "must not be used as a text in any of our Catholic schools and is not to be displayed, sold, or distributed in any of our churches". This was, he said, because the book "presents Christ, the Trinity and Redemption in terms which cannot be reconciled with the doctrine of the Church".[15]

A laudatory foreword to Morwood's book had been provided by the ubiquitous Thomas Groome who wrote: "He [Morwood] is convinced, and rightly so, that the 'package' of Catholicism we received from the previous era is no longer adequate to the challenges of this age. To refashion Catholicism to meet the challenges of this new era requires imagination and courage, and Morwood demonstrates both ... *Tomorrow's Catholic* invites us to take some bold steps in the right direction".

In response to Archbishop Pell's action and to a similar move at the time by the Vatican against Fr Paul Collins' book *Papal Power*, the Australian Conference of Leaders of Religious Institutes (ACLRI) issued a statement commenting on such "censorship". Fr Kevin Dance CP, President of ACLRI, said "Dialogue, not condemnation is the hallmark of an adult Church. It is important we avoid a climate of suspicion within the Australian Church".

Fr Dance added, "New times reveal new insights and result in fresh expressions of our faith. When differences occur in insight or expression, theologians and Bishops alike — indeed all men and women of the Church — are bound by the same values of humility, honesty, patience, respect for the other and a love for the Church".[16]

However, it was one thing for theologians to delve creatively into the mysteries of faith and share their thoughts with colleagues in learned journals. It was another for Fathers Morwood, Collins and others to air their versions of the faith at gatherings in parishes and dioceses with an appearance of official endorsement, or even in the secular media.

Prior to Archbishop Pell's rejection of *Tomorrow's Catholic*, Father Morwood was given red carpet treatment in the Ballarat Diocese "facilitating" its 1997 Diocesan Assembly as a member of a team of three including Fr Frank Andersen MSC, and involved in the Ballarat Diocese Adult Faith Education Program, with *Tomorrow's Catholic* a key reference that was said to provide "a significant challenge to the philosophical and cultural underpinnings of contemporary Australian Catholicism".

In November 1997, Fr Morwood was the keynote speaker at a seminar day in the Ballarat Diocese titled "Re-imagining Our Catholic Culture: Exploring themes from the Catholic Education Conference of Victoria 1997".[17]

In 1999, Archbishop Pell announced that another of Morwood's books, *God is Near: Understanding a Changing Church*, would not be sold at the Catholic Bookshop in Melbourne — the now Mr Morwood having left the priesthood three months earlier. Ms Maria Rohr, speaking for the book's publisher, Spectrum, said "I am very, very angry. This issue is out of control". She added, "People use [*God is Near*] in a big way in discussion groups" where she said it helped them appreciate the meaning of the changes in attitude and practice in Catholic life.[18]

Another of Archbishop Pell's initiatives was in the field of Australian Catholic higher education with the official opening of the John Paul II Institute for Marriage and Family in July 2001. The Institute would provide a full range of degrees, ranging from one-year graduate diplomas to higher research and course work degrees in the areas of marriage, family and bio-ethics.[19]

The Institute was part of a growing worldwide network connected with the Pontifical Institute for Studies on Marriage and the Family established by John Paul II in 1982 through his Apostolic Constitution *Magnum Matrimonii Sacramentum*.

Archbishop Pell said that the Melbourne Institute would be "working in conjunction with the John Paul II Pontifical Institute for Studies of Marriage and the Family around the world and with the University of Notre Dame in Perth", and would "provide theological and pastoral training for priests and religious, teachers, catechists, pastoral workers, nurses and physicians, and lay people interested in deepening their understanding of the issues touching marriage, family and the culture of life in our world today".

Dr Anthony Fisher OP, Episcopal Vicar for Health Care for the Archdiocese of Melbourne, and an internationally recognised expert on marriage, family and bio-ethical issues, was appointed as Director with the permanent faculty of the Institute to be complemented by visiting lecturers from Asia and the Pacific, Europe and the United States. (Dr Fisher would later be appointed an auxiliary bishop in Sydney).

The John Paul II Institute was part of a growing Catholic theological complex that Archbishop Pell set up in the heart of Melbourne, sharing its facilities with the Catholic Pastoral Formation Centre and the Catholic Theological College. It would collaborate closely with the Archdiocesan Respect Life Office, which promotes the Gospel of Life in parishes, schools and hospitals in the Melbourne Archdiocese.

The Institute was located close to the recently set up St Patrick's Campus of the Australian Catholic University (combining the two previous Melbourne campuses in Ascot Vale and Oakleigh), St Patrick's Cathedral, the major Catholic hospitals, the Catholic Education Office, Catholic Social Services, the relocated Corpus Christi Seminary and various offices of the Archdiocese of Melbourne.

Those teaching at the Institute were to be mandated by the Church — in line with John Paul II's Apostolic Constitution on Catholic higher education *Ex Corde Ecclesiae*.

Sydney

On 26 March 2001 came the stunning news — for both supporters and critics — that Archbishop Pell had been chosen to succeed the 77-year-old Cardinal Edward Clancy as Archbishop of Sydney. Many considered Dr Pell's less than five years in Melbourne to have been insufficient for him to cement the reforms he had begun. Evidently, the Holy See believed the high-profile Archbishop would have greater impact nationally as leader of the country's senior archdiocese.

The Holy See's close interest in the condition of Australian Catholicism had been evident in the content the *Statement of Conclusions*.

In an interview with this writer for the American monthly, *Catholic World Report*, Archbishop Pell commented, "I think the Statement is a fair and accurate description of what's going on in Australia — but a bit understated".[20]

This estimate contrasted with that of Cardinal Clancy.[21] During an interview on ABC Radio on 1 April, just days after Archbishop Pell's appointment was announced, Cardinal Clancy referred to what he called a "spy network" within the Church. He suggested that the Australian bishops had been undermined at the Synod of Oceania by unofficial reports sent to Rome by people critical of the state of the Church. "I came away", he said, "feeling that our brethren in Rome didn't fully understand the situation in real life as we have it here. I would think that this group [of critics] did exercise an undue influence in forming opinions and convictions over there. I think that was the big shortcoming of the meeting".

But if more bishops had taken up legitimate complaints about abuses and shortcomings in the first place, the *Statement of Conclusions* might not have been needed.

Many media reports and commentaries on the appointment were predictably hostile, with two TV channels inviting a homosexual activist, an outspoken radical opponent and Dr Paul Collins to provide responses. They obliged with one predicting Archbishop Pell would

Archbishop George Pell with Cardinal Edward Clancy at a press conference following Dr Pell's appointment to Sydney

drag Sydney's Catholics back to the Middle Ages.

Chris McGillion, religion correspondent for *The Sydney Morning Herald*, (the liberal sister daily of the Melbourne *Age*) referred to Dr Pell as an "arch-conservative" who had "drawn criticism for his hardline positions" on the Serrano 'art' exhibition (and its blasphemous "Piss Christ" photo of a crucifix in a jar of urine), "refusing to serve communion to openly homosexual Catholics" and angering feminist groups by opposing access to IVF programs for single women.[22]

The Sydney Morning Herald commented in an editorial,[23] "The Vatican clearly believes that what Dr Pell has wrought in Melbourne is what Sydney also requires". The move, it said, reflected "a conservative Pope's desire to install a strong, conservative representative of the Church in Australia". Dr Pell, it continued, "fits the mould of a church leader impatient with those who question papal authority and doctrine and unbendingly opposed to change on such issues as the place of gays in the Church, women's ordination, the celibacy of priests and contraception".

Archbishop Hickey of Perth, however, welcomed the appointment, describing Archbishop Pell as a "strong leader" who would bring to a head the many issues polarising the Church in Australia and help resolve them.[24]

These issues, he said, included "Cafeteria Catholicism" versus Church authority, calls for so-called democratisation of the Church as opposed to the rightful role of its hierarchy, a trend towards forms of pantheism as opposed to seeing God as Creator of the universe, seeing sexuality as self-expression rather than affirming its true place in committed love and marriage, and a loss of understanding of what happens in the Church's liturgy. On every one of these issues, said Archbishop Hickey, Archbishop Pell "stands four-square with the Church's teaching".

The new Archbishop's media skills were evident during interviews at St Mary's Cathedral, Sydney, on 27 March following the announcement of his appointment. He told one questioner, "There will be no new Pellian documents here. I will only be teaching squarely what Christ and the Catholic Church teach and I will present those consistently and with compassion — the cards will fall as they do".[25]

On 10 May 2001, Dr Pell was installed as the eighth Archbishop of Sydney in St Mary's Cathedral and during his homily, he set out his priorities for the archdiocese.[26]

Perhaps the most significant point made — in light of attempts in other dioceses to cope with the clergy shortfall by promoting lay-led liturgies — was Archbishop Pell's emphasis on the need for more priests. "The one constant in all Catholic history," he stressed, "is the need for priests, for vocations to the ministerial priesthood. Our Lord himself appointed the twelve, called forth the shepherds, the fishers of men. St Paul underlined the importance of ambassadors for Christ. Without priests our parishes will wither and die.

"A priestless parish is a contradiction in terms, because there is no parish without the sacraments, without Baptism, Eucharist, Reconciliation. We should pray that in the years ahead a sufficient number of young men will be on a wavelength that enables them to hear Christ's call to the priesthood, to join those gallant priests expending themselves in faithful service and prayer in the Archdiocese and elsewhere".

Archbishop Pell would soon be launching or fostering a series of positive initiatives.

Begun in 2001, with his support, was Carnivale Christi, a religious drama festival organised by young Catholics, aimed at promoting Christian culture through various art forms like music, theatre, film and painting. This would become a regular feature in years to come in several major cities.[27]

During an address to the NSW Press Forum, Parliament House, Sydney, in March 2002, Archbishop Pell presented the case for an uncompromising orthodoxy and its greater appeal for the young. He pointed out that "the sociological evidence from Europe, the USA and Australia clearly demonstrates that the more conservative religious groups attract greater numbers of followers. It is groups which resist compromise who flourish most successfully in a climate of uncertainty".[28]

This claim, "that religious conservatism has a monopoly on growth, particularly among young people, is both surprising and unwelcome to a significant section of élite Christian opinion. Older Catholic leaders, who struggled faithfully to implement 'Vatican II' and liberate their co-religionists from the constraints of 'the fifties', have sometimes simply rejected the claim as untrue. Others are sad; a few vow never to turn back whatever the sociology".

The Archbishop continued, "Generally speaking, liberal Catholicism in Australia has been unable to inspire young people to join it. The public protest meetings following the *Statement of Conclusions ...* were attended by few if any under the age of fifty. Almost as disturbing is the fact that supporters of the Pope have not done spectacularly better among the young. However, the minority of young Catholic adults who are enthusiastic participants are strongly orthodox".

Archbishop Pell's international stature was evident when, on 20 April, John Paul II announced the setting up of a new body representing the world's English-speaking bishops' conferences, called the Vox Clara Committee. Its role, he said, was "to assist and advise the Congregation for Divine Worship and the Discipline of the Sacraments in fulfilling its responsibilities with regard to the English translations of liturgical texts".[29]

Following publication of the third Latin edition of the Roman Missal in March 2002 as the official standard for the liturgy, the next step was to make vernacular language editions available — including English ones.

The Committee, consisting of 12 bishops from such nations as the US, Canada, England, Ireland, Ghana, India, the Philippines and Australia, chose Archbishop George Pell as its chairman.

John Paul II directed that this Committee ensure "the texts of the Roman Rite are accurately translated in accordance with the norms of the Instruction *Liturgiam Authenticam*" and the process of completing an English translation of the new Roman Missal is completed "as soon as possible".

In a statement on 24 April, Archbishop Pell emphasised "the absolute need for translations of the Roman *editiones typicae*" to be "precise, theologically faithful and effectively proclaimable".

During 2002, he established a Catholic Chaplaincy Team at Sydney University aimed at bolstering the Catholic presence on campus through the setting up of a team of people committed to providing activities and support for Catholic students.[30]

Among the activities were studies of Scripture and weekly public forums or lectures by guest speakers on topics of interest. Their aim was to promote and defend the faith in a secular environment. A team of four priests — all noted for their orthodoxy — was formed to assist the Chaplaincy with Masses and confessions.

This was followed in 2005 by the launch of a five-year program to extend the Sydney Archdiocese's existing presence at the University of Sydney to other university campuses with at least two chaplains at each large campus. The overall aim was to build a Catholic culture among tertiary students.[31]

Stephen Lawrence, a former premiership footballer for the Victorian Australian Rules club Hawthorn, was appointed the Convener of Tertiary Chaplains for the Archdiocese of Sydney.

The new chaplaincy strategy was aimed at enhancing and strengthening the presence of a Catholic leadership at each campus while reaching more students and retaining them. An additional position at Sydney University was to be a general schools' co-ordinator, to bridge the gap between secondary schools and the university.

Every Wednesday afternoon the chaplains take up a position in a prominent place on campus and make a visible presence in the name of the Church, with a large picture of the Pope, an icon, the presence of a priest in habit, a small table covered in promotional material for World Youth Day or events on campus, and a Bible and Catechism.

Earlier, on 28 September 2003, the Pope named Archbishop George Pell as one of 30 new cardinals from around the world. This was anticipated since leadership of the Sydney Archdiocese usually carries with it a red hat.

A cause of further rejoicing was the announcement by Benedict XVI on 21 August 2005 that Sydney would be hosting World Youth Day in 2008. He later confirmed that he would be attending.

Cardinal Pell had presented a strong case with the Holy See for WYD to come to Australia in the hope, as he put it, of breaking "through the fog of apathy and disinterest that surrounds institutionalised religion in the West" — and particularly in Australia.

Since his posting to Sydney, Cardinal Pell has reactivated the seminary along the lines he charted in Melbourne with a similarly promising increase in numbers.

Other "John Paul II bishops"

With the departure of Archbishop Pell from Melbourne to Sydney in 2001, there was a major vacancy to be filled. Auxiliary Bishop Denis Hart was named on 11 May as the interim Diocesan Administrator and it was widely expected he would be the new Archbishop, given his close association with Archbishop Pell, his solid orthodoxy and high qualifications in liturgy. This was confirmed from Rome on 22 June.

In a media statement on 23 June, Archbishop Hart set out his intentions as Church leader. "I will work hard," he said, "to promote unity of faith in the Catholic tradition with Jesus Christ as its centre. I will work energetically to gather the Church in Melbourne around Pope John Paul II in the Universal Church ... Archbishop Pell has provided Melbourne with a strong focus on Jesus Christ, with clear teaching, gifted administration and availability to all. For all Melburnians I thank him for his vision and leadership".[32]

Since 2001, Archbishop Hart has continued the reforms begun by his predecessor in the seminary and in Catholic education — notably continuation and extension of the new religious education texts — while taking initiatives of his own.

These included the new *Sexuality Directives for the Archdiocese of Melbourne* in January 2002. The Archbishop clarified the Church's role in teaching on matters of faith and morals, reminding parents and educators that it was a "task first and foremost to parents" and that "the role of the school is to facilitate parents" in their task. He emphasised the sense of delicacy needed especially in the area of Christian education in sexuality.[33]

Catholic schools were asked to "review all areas of the curriculum" related to education in sexuality to ensure these were "formative of chastity and respect for the sacredness of human life and the dignity of marriage".

In May 2002 Archbishop Hart launched a two-year program based on John Paul II's Apostolic Letter *Novo Millennio Ineunte* (2001). Titled "Contemplate — Launch Out: Linking Prayer and Mission in the light of *Novo Millennio Ineunte*", it was placed under the patronage of Our Lady of Perpetual Help and, in the words of Archbishop Hart, aimed "to apply the wonderful teaching of Pope John Paul ll's Apostolic Letter, *Novo Millennio Ineunte* to the Archdiocese of Melbourne". [34]

Responding to further papal teaching, in this case John Paul II's request in his Apostolic Letter *Rosarium Virginis Mariae* to celebrate the period from October 2002 to October 2003 as the Year of the Rosary, the Melbourne Archdiocese produced a new program to foster the Rosary in Catholic primary and secondary schools.[35]

On his return from Rome, following the Australian bishops' 2004 ad limina, Archbishop Hart circularised his priests with the reminder, "As Archbishop I ask all our priests and communities to follow the approved liturgical texts and rites with the vestments and ceremonies given there without change. I would be grateful if you could emphasise this with those helping to prepare liturgies in your parishes, colleges, schools and communities".[36]

Archbishop Hart's strong liturgical credentials made him a logical choice as the Australian Bishops' representative on ICEL — the International Commission on English in the Liturgy — which has been working on a new translation of the Missal.

In his homily given at the end-of-year Mass for the National Civic Council at Our Lady of Victories' Basilica, Camberwell, in 2004 Archbishop Hart spoke on the theme of John Paul II and the Year of the Eucharist.[37]

The Pope, he said, wished "to reinforce our faith in the Eucharist, which has been weakened in the last thirty years" and "to open ourselves to the full dimensions of the Eucharist".

The Archbishop drew attention to "one aspect", which the Pope wanted "particularly emphasised", namely, the need "to cultivate a lively awareness of Christ's Real Presence, both in the celebration of the Mass and in the worship of the Eucharist outside Mass". This meant a further emphasis on "the importance of silence in Mass and Eucharistic Adoration".

Adelaide

The appointments of bishops more in touch with the needs of the Church continued with the transfer of Bishop Philip Wilson of Wollongong, NSW, to Adelaide as its new Archbishop in 2001.

His task was perhaps the most difficult of those appointed, given the long period — since the end of the Council — in which Adelaide had been run on "spirit of Vatican II" lines. Those who had overseen or promoted this approach were still well entrenched and many of the clergy and religious possessed this mind-set.

On 3 December 2001, Archbishop Wilson was installed as the new Archbishop of Adelaide, following a period of 12 months as Coadjutor Archbishop. No doubt he had ample opportunity to observe the state of the Archdiocese at first hand.

Prior to his installation, Archbishop Wilson, in an interview with Matthew Abraham, editor of *The Southern Cross* — Adelaide's archdiocesan periodical — set out the principles that would guide him in the future.[38]

"During his 12 months as Archbishop-in-waiting," said Mr Abraham, "he has often been told, sometimes in a good-natured way, sometimes not, that he must learn the 'Adelaide way of doing things' as archbishop".

The Archbishop offered the following response. "While some people," he said, "who have entrenched positions may say you have to accept the Adelaide way of doing things, there may be an element of that, but they may also accept that these things evolve too. That the Adelaide way of doing things depends on whoever is archbishop at the time".

Aware of recent efforts in Adelaide to promote Basic Ecclesial Communities as the way forward for the Church, the Archbishop made clear that these kinds of initiatives should defer to the central role of the parish. "I think the notion of a parish based within a particular geographical region with a community centred upon the celebration of the Eucharist and the sacraments is not a dinosaur by any means but in fact it would seem to me like someone once said about the family, that the parish should be a haven in a heartless world".

During an address to teachers and trainee teachers at the start of the 2004 school year, Archbishop Wilson reminded his audience of the Church's educational priorities.[39]

He pointed out that the main focus of a Catholic education was not primarily Year 12 exam success or university entrance. "What we are concerned with is what happens to people when they die," he said. "We want people to be able to develop their relationship with God and with the Church while they're alive and then to be prepared for eternal life".

At the time of writing, it appears Archbishop Wilson has had only limited success in countering the influence of Adelaide's well-entrenched liberal establishment.

Armidale

Among significant appointments to smaller rural dioceses has been the Belgian-born Fr Luc Matthys who became Bishop of Armidale in northern New South Wales in 1999. He had spent many years as a priest in South Africa before moving to Melbourne and serving as a parish priest before his appointment by Archbishop Pell as Administrator of St Patrick's Cathedral.

In July 2001, Bishop Matthys launched a *Faith and Practice* program of "Systematic instruction in the faith".[40] In his letter addressed "to all the faithful of his diocese, especially priests and teachers", he outlined an initiative to re-evangelise through the schools and parish churches, using the *Catechism of the Catholic Church* as the point of reference. The program would run for four years, using one of the four sections of the Catechism each year.

He called for "a concerted and common effort by all priests, catechists, teachers, and parents" so that the same subject/theme would be given at each Sunday Mass.

The first phase of the program was completed in November 2001 and followed by an evaluation process, with forms sent to all parish priests, religious houses and religious education co-ordinators. The overall return rate was 73 per cent, with the results collated into a report for Bishop Matthys, later published in the diocesan paper.[41]

Bishop Matthys had earlier met with his *Faith and Practice* task group which found the program had been "well received overall" and involved a high level of participation. It was decided to make an earlier start to part two of the program on "The Creed" on 9 June 2002.

Reinforcing the work of *Faith and Practice* was the launch in 2005 of a program to promote Sunday observance based on John Paul II's Apostolic Letter of 1998, *Dies Domini*, "On Keeping the Lord's Day Holy".[42]

Lismore

Another welcome appointment was that of Fr Geoffrey Jarrett, a former Anglican vicar and Tasmanian parish priest, to the Diocese of Lismore in northern New South Wales.

Like Bishop Matthys, Bishop Jarrett has been an active member of the Australian Confraternity of Catholic Clergy, an organisation of orthodox priests noted for their strong support for the Pope and Church teachings.

Since his installation on 12 December 2001, Bishop Jarrett has been tireless in setting out the Catholic faith in his homilies and pastoral letters, referring to Sunday Mass obligation, the Eucharist as a sacrifice, the need for sound catechetics and a greater sense of sin. He has called for promotion of priestly vocations while emphasising the indispensable nature of the priesthood.[43]

"There can never be a substitute for a priest," he said, "and there cannot be a parish without him. A priestless Church would no longer be a Church; it would but die away. Because the priest is meant to model his life on the mystery of the Lord's cross, and to stand among the people sacramentally in the Lord's own place — 'another Christ' ... I will be doing all in my power to seek and encourage vocations and, as a bishop, I will know no joy like that of bestowing the priesthood on those generous men who respond".

In a Pastoral Letter in June 2004, Bishop Jarrett called on parishes to be places where the Liturgy is "celebrated with reverence and beauty as befits the mysteries of faith; to be the place where everyone can hear the faith taught authoritatively as the Church has handed it down to us from the Apostles".[44]

He welcomed the resurgence of Eucharistic adoration in the diocese and expressed his full support for "every effort made by priests and local communities to foster regularly, even frequently, these very valuable times of prayerful adoration focussed on the Person of Jesus Christ, abiding with us in the Blessed Sacrament of the altar". This practice, he said, should also be encouraged in schools.

The religion texts begun in Melbourne by Archbishop Pell and later continued in Sydney, are now being used in both the Armidale and Lismore dioceses.

Other appointments of note in recent years have included several new auxiliary bishops in large archdioceses, with Bishops Anthony Fisher and Julian Porteous in Sydney, Bishops Mark Coleridge and Christopher Prowse in Melbourne, and Bishop Donald Sproxton in Perth.

In June 2006, in a widely welcomed move, it was announced that Benedict XVI had appointed Bishop Coleridge as the new Archbishop of Canberra-Goulburn to succeed Archbishop Francis Carroll.

Endnotes

1. *Knightlife*, February/March 2002.
2. Archbishop Barry Hickey, *Pastoral Letter on 25th Anniversary of 'Humanae Vitae'*, July 1993.
3. Brian Peachey, "Pregnancy assistance", *AD2000*, April 2005, p. 15.
4. Archbishop Barry Hickey, *Pastoral Letter on Christian Marriage*, 9 February 2003.
5. Archbishop Barry Hickey, *Priests and Eucharistic Liturgy*, March 1995.
6. Archbishop Hickey's letter to his priests, *AD2000*, March 2004, p. 4.

Bishops Luc Matthys (Armidale) and Geoffrey Jarrett (Lismore)

7. "New Catholic radio program to start in WA", *AD2000*, March 2001, p. 12.
8. "Archbishop Hickey presents Papal teachings", *AD2000*, April 2004, p. 4.
9. *The Record*, 17 November, 2005.
10. Bishop George Pell, "Issues facing Australian Catholicism", *AD2000*, November 1988, pp. 7-8.
11. Msgr Peter Elliott, "New texts the key to reshaping religious education", *AD2000*, June 1998, pp. 3-4.
12. Martin Daly, "Return to the dark ages?", *The Sunday Age*, 23 May 1999.
13. Statement by the Catholic Archbishop of Melbourne Dr George Pell, addressing the issue of homosexuals who request Holy Communion, St Patrick's Cathedral, Melbourne, 31 May 1998.
14. Archbishop George Pell, *On Life and Love: Pastoral Letter for the 30th Anniversary of 'Humanae Vitae'*, 25 July 1998.
15. Michael Gilchrist, "Basic questions for today's Church", *AD2000*, May 1998, pp. 3-4.
16. Australian Conference of Leaders of Religious Institutes, "Dialogue — the hallmark of an adult Church", 19 March 1998.
17. Ballarat Diocesan Pastoral Planning Office, "Shaping Our Church", Diocesan Assembly, November 14-15, 1997; Ballarat Diocese, "Re-imagining Our Catholic Culture: Exploring themes from the Catholic Education Conference of Victoria 1997", Damascus College, Ballarat, 3 November 1997.
18. Fergus Shiel, "Pell bans second book by ex-priest", *The Age*, 10 March 1999.
19. AD2000 Report, "John Paul II Institute for Marriage and Family to open in July", *AD2000*, April 2001, p. 3.
20. Interview with Michael Gilchrist, *Catholic World Report*, May 2000.
21. "Vatican signals continuation of reform process", *AD2000*, May 2001, pp. 3-4.
22. *The Sydney Morning Herald*, 28 March 2001.
23. Ibid.
24. *The Record* (Perth), 30 March 2001.
25. "Vatican signals continuation of reform process", *AD2000*, May 2001, p. 3-4.
26. Ibid.
27. Angela Smith, "Carnivale Christi: an inspiring display of Christian culture", *AD2000*, July 2001, p. 8.
28. Archbishop George Pell, "Catholicism in Australia: facing the challenge of Western secularism", *AD2000*, May 2002, pp. 6-7.
29. Michael Gilchrist, "New English Missal: Archbishop Pell to chair international committee", *AD2000*, June 2002, p. 3.
30. Robert Haddad, "Sydney initiative to strengthen Catholic influence at university", *AD2000*, June 2002, p. 7.
31. Stephen Lawrence, "Cardinal Pell's program for a Catholic culture at Sydney's universities", *AD2000*, August 2005, p. 6.
32. "Melbourne's new Archbishop receives Pallium from John Paul II", *AD2000*, August 2001, p. 3.

33. Archbishop Denis Hart, *Sexuality Directives for the Archdiocese of Melbourne*, January 2002.
34. Archbishop Denis Hart, *Contemplate — Launch Out: Linking Prayer and Mission in the Light of Novo Millennio Ineunte*, 24 May 2002.
35. Archdiocese of Melbourne, *Teaching Companion: Year of the Rosary 2003.*
36. Michael Gilchrist, "Australian Bishops' ad limina: strong leadership needed to confront secularism", *AD2000*, May 2004, p. 6.
37. Archbishop Denis Hart, Homily, National Civic Council Mass, Our Lady of Victories Basilica, Camberwell, 1 December 2004.
38. *The Southern Cross* (Adelaide), p. 9.
39. "Archbishop Wilson's challenge for educators", *AD2000*, March 2004, p. 2.
40. "Systematic instruction in the faith program to be launched in July", *AD2000*, May 2001, p. 5.
41. *Catholic Viewpoint* (Armidale), 17 February 2002.
42. Bishop Luc Matthys, "Armidale Diocese promotes Sunday observance", *AD2000*, October 2005, p. 9.
43. Bishop Geoffrey Jarrett, Homily, Mass of Installation, Lismore, 12 December 2001.
44. Bishop Geoffrey Jarrett, *Pastoral Letter to the Clergy, Religious and Lay People of Lismore Diocese*, June 2004.

Chapter Ten

Seminaries

One of the few positive growth areas in Australian Catholicism over the past decade — thanks to the initiatives of several bishops — has been in seminary formation. While the increases are not usually large enough to offset deaths and retirements, the young men being ordained are consistently orthodox and have had a beneficial impact in their dioceses.

The number of seminarians worldwide increased significantly following the advent of John Paul II, from 64,000 in 1978 to 113,000 in 2004, although their distribution remains uneven, with most Western nations continuing their post-1970s decline.[1]

In Australia, the clergy shortage has produced two radically different responses in recent decades.

In some dioceses, there is still talk of priestless parishes, restructurings and the need to organise more lay-led liturgies with these developments even described as the work of the Holy Spirit. This approach has become a self-fulfilling prophecy as seminary numbers keep falling and priests retire, die or leave the priesthood.

This was to be expected. If the priesthood is devalued when lay people are seemingly presented as substitutes, who would wish to enter a seminary with all the sacrifices that entails?

In fact, most young men considering the priesthood these days have seen John Paul II — and later Benedict XVI — as their model.

They are better informed about the divided state of the Church than their predecessors and know which dioceses offer realistic prospects for an effective ministry. Where "spirit of Vatican II" religious and clergy hold sway, there is little to attract potential vocations.

But where a bishop teaches the faith without apology, supports orthodoxy, reforms the seminary and upholds the indispensable role of the priesthood, young men, not surprisingly, have responded in greater numbers. This was the case firstly in the small Diocese of Wagga Wagga, NSW, where Bishop William Brennan opened his own seminary, and later in Perth, Melbourne and Sydney.

The situation in Australia before the reforms were begun was outlined by a visiting American parish priest from Texas, Fr Timothy E. Deeter, who was in Australia for a number of Marian conferences in April 1994. While here, he took the opportunity to observe at close hand the condition of the seminaries and the views of seminarians or young men wishing to enter them.[2]

"It is not unusual for me to meet one or two vocations prospects when I speak at conferences in the United States. I was not prepared, however, for the number of young Australian men who came to me to discuss their possible calling to the priesthood — about two dozen of them! These were friendly, personable, devout men in their twenties, who were ready to enter the seminary. And all of them had the same question: which seminary?

"This question was not asked out of naivete or ignorance. Each man expressed his personal concern about liberal leanings in the local seminaries. These men already had done their research — vocation weekends, seminary visits, and discussions with seminarian friends. Two men had previously entered seminaries and then dropped out after a month or so.

"As it turned out, I was able to glean first-hand information about preparation for the priesthood in Australia. In one city we were housed at the local seminary, while in another I had lunch and extensive conversation with a group of seminarians. And even though I have my own war-stories to tell, having survived my 'training' in one of America's most liberal schools of theology, I was nevertheless surprised and saddened to learn what is happening in some of Australia's seminaries.

"Australian seminarians who kneel during their prayers or who genuflect to the Blessed Sacrament are, in some places, reprimanded for making a 'political statement.' Those who fast on Wednesdays or Fridays are advised not to do so, since their fasting is considered 'divisive' at table. Some who choose to receive Holy Communion on the tongue are questioned about their choice and told to 'think about it.'

"From reports I received, devotion to Our Lord in the Blessed Sacrament is non-existent, despite the advice of countless saintly spiritual directors saying a priest needs daily time in adoration of the Eucharistic Lord ...

"When I was in the seminary, those of us who wore clerical dress on occasions were tolerated but not condemned. An Australian priest at one of the seminaries, however, publicly told the students that Father Stephen Barham and I were 'fundamentalists' because we wore clerical dress and were involved with the Marian Conference.

"This is what I learned about liberals while I was in the seminary, and it seems to be the same in Australia: liberals want everyone to be 'free' — to believe as they do. One is not free to practise traditional devotions unharassed. Those students who meet on their own to pray the rosary, or to conduct their own holy hours, are oftentimes mocked by priests as well as fellow students. Those who exercise their canonical right of choice of methods of receiving the Host, are summoned before an authority figure and challenged.

"I strongly believe that the Church has no shortage of vocations: what we have is a problem in many seminaries, Australian and American. And the seeds of the many future problems in the priesthood and in the Church are being planted in these 'seed plots' (which is what 'seminary' means) — a disdain for or lack of commitment to the official prayer of the Church, an absence of strong faith in the Eucharist, a tendency to belittle or altogether ignore Our Lady, an indifference to the public witness of clerical dress, and a passing-over of the Church's rich tradition of forms of personal prayer in favour of New Age faddism".

Problems like these would be gradually overcome during the 1990s, thanks to the leadership of several Australian bishops. Subsequently, Archbishop Hickey invited Fr Deeter to establish a vocational residence where young men are guided in discerning their vocation.

American situation

The seminary situation in the United States resembles Australia's and has been extensively researched. In the US, there is a clear link between orthodox dioceses and seminaries and larger numbers of recruits for the priesthood.

The Diocese of Peoria, Illinois, for example, was successfully "repriested" thanks to the leadership of Bishop John Myers.[3] In the period from 1990-1992, Peoria, which then had just over 230,000 Catholics, ordained 33 men to the priesthood — one more than the neighbouring Archdiocese of Chicago (then under the liberal leadership of Cardinal Bernadin), which had ten times more Catholics. Los Angeles, which had three million Catholics, ordained only four more than Peoria during the same period.

Why did such a relatively small diocese have so many vocations?

From the outset, Bishop Myers made no apologies for even the most challenging of Catholic teachings, and with three strongly-worded pastoral documents — one on abortion, another on the Eucharist, and the third on catechetics — he made clear his total identity with John Paul II.

Bishop Myers attributed the results in Peoria to "grace" and a refusal on his part to soften the Church's celibacy requirement. "I found", he said, "that rather than caving in to the culture, holding the ideal high gets young people's attention. I see among the religious communities that those who have maintained the highest expectations and demand the most have more vocations. With our seminarians, we just don't pull punches. We expect them to be chaste, we expect them to love the Church, and we have built the program around love for — a personal relationship with — Jesus Christ, especially in the sacraments, love for the Blessed Mother and devotion to the Blessed Mother, and love for the Church, especially the Holy Father and bishops".

A similar approach has worked in other American dioceses.

In Arlington, Virginia, the Vocations Director, Father James Gould, offered as the formula for success, "Unswerving allegiance to the Pope and magisterial teaching; perpetual adoration of the Blessed Sacrament in parishes, with an emphasis on praying for vocations;

and a strong effort by a significant number of diocesan priests who extend themselves to help young men remain open to the Lord's will in their lives".[4]

An in-depth study of statistics from the 2003 and 2004 editions of *The Official Catholic Directory* for each of the United States' 176 dioceses determined the ratios of seminarians to Catholic population.[5]

Successful seminaries were linked for the most part with strong, orthodox episcopal leadership, the witness of devout, enthusiastic clergy, focus on the indispensable role of the priest, effective programs in schools and parishes, and spiritual practices such as Eucharistic adoration.

The twelve most successful dioceses are relatively small, all bar one having fewer than 100,000 Catholics, suggesting that smaller size enables the impact of strong leadership to be more directly felt and regular interaction between a bishop and his seminarians to occur.

Topping the list was the diocese of Lincoln, Nebraska, led by Bishop Fabian Bruskewitz. Roughly the size of Australia's Rockhampton or Ballarat dioceses in Catholic population, Lincoln had 35 seminarians in training in 2004 (38 in 2005) — a ratio of one seminarian for 2,555 Catholics. In recent years, Ballarat, Rockhampton and several other comparable Australian dioceses would be lucky to have more than one or two at the seminary at any given time.

Of the medium sized dioceses, Denver, Colorado, with 380,739 Catholics, and led by Archbishop Charles Chaput, had the best ratio, placing it 14th out of 176 with 77 seminarians. To put this in perspective, Denver is about the same size as Perth, Australia's most vocation-rich larger diocese. In the academic year 2005-06, there were 14 ordinations for Denver, the largest number since the 1960s and the third largest number in the United States, including dioceses ten times Denver's size.

Of the largest dioceses, Chicago, led by Cardinal Francis George, is by far the most successful with 336 seminarians for its 2.4 million Catholics. Its numbers have quadrupled since the solidly orthodox Cardinal Francis George replaced the liberal Cardinal Joseph Bernadin. On the other hand, the more liberal Los Angeles, with over four million Catholics, has 77 seminarians.

The impact of strong, orthodox leadership could not be clearer.

Orthodoxy

Another positive trend connected with the above has been the orthodoxy of most seminarians and young priests in the United States and Australia. This is obviously the result of orthodox bishops and seminaries attracting the most recruits in recent years.

One American seminarian recently summed up what he saw as the typical attributes of his contemporaries.[6] His description could easily apply to many of today's seminarians in Australia.

"My brothers and I", he said, "have been surgeons, school teachers, health care professionals, bartenders, musicians, marketing executives, retailers, farmers, lawyers, architects and military officers. Some of our older brothers are widowed with children; others have been in religious orders for some years. Well over half of new theologate seminarians have had a career.

"We have seen the world from the inside and have made an unsentimental assessment of its condition. We have seen family cohesion dissolve before our eyes, and have witnessed galloping violence, materialism, and radical individualism erode our culture. We have watched in dismay as an aggressive iconoclasm has replaced traditional notions of beauty, purity and nobility.

"It is our conviction that the only serious response to the unravelling of our moral fabric is a committed hope in the person of Jesus Christ and the Church he founded.

"We have a deep distrust of anything that smacks of relativism. We have become suspicious of those who appear to arrogate to themselves the authority not to find truth, but to create truth. We want boundaries of right and wrong, and are tired of people telling us to do whatever we feel like. As Bishop Allen H. Vigneron of Sacred Heart Seminary said in a May 1999 interview in *Crisis* magazine, for most young seminarians, 'assent to the whole range of Church doctrine is not a return or a move back; it's new, a novelty they find bracing. Integral Catholic faith is for them a fresh discovery'.

"We have lost our faith in an unreflective trust of one's own emotions and their unchecked authority over our activity. As sons of the

Church, we look to the Magisterium and to the Church's historical and spiritual treasures to fill the void of authority left by those who tout self-affirmation at all costs. We are unashamed to proclaim our explicit and emphatic loyalty to the Pope and to the bishops in union with him and are more inclined to emphasize catechesis, vigorous spiritual direction, cultivation of 'manly' virtues, and an appreciation for spiritual classics.

"We place little faith in an unswerving obedience to one's own conscience that, practically speaking, disregards Church teachings, and we exhibit a greater willingness to obey and to take radical steps to form our consciences according to the mind and heart of the Church and not according to any predetermined slant.

"Finally, we place great importance on the rituals of the Church and on the mystical aspects of our Faith. This is not an exclusivist approach; we embrace the renewed sense of *communio* emphasised by the Second Vatican Council and in no way wish to detach the Mass from its impact on Catholic life. The Eucharist is the '*sacramentum caritatis*,' the bedrock of our life of charity and remains, as the Catechism states, intrinsically linked to our concern for the poor (CCC 1397).

"Our aim, though, is nothing new: to preach the Good News, to teach men and women how to live freely as children of God, and to cherish the collected wisdom of our fathers, especially our fathers in faith. We are not trying to turn back the clock, to stifle change, or to reverse the Second Vatican Council. Indeed, we invoke that very Vatican Council in our efforts to bring the Christian message back into the world, and we energetically support the great 'new evangelisation' that will transform the twenty-first century".

The same situation applies among the younger, more recently ordained priests.

A survey of American and Puerto Rican Catholic priests conducted between June and October 2002 by the *Los Angeles Times* was later analysed by Fr Brian Harrison OS. About 5,000 of America's approximately 45,000 priests had been asked to respond to a detailed questionnaire.[7]

Australian born and raised a non-Catholic, Fr Brian Harrison is an outstanding academic theologian who teaches in Puerto Rico. He was converted to Catholicism, impressed by the consistency in *Humanae Vitae* with the Church's traditional teaching and was ordained a priest by Pope John Paul II in 1985.

Fr Harrison's analysis revealed that younger priests ordained during the past 20 years were more orthodox doctrinally and less dissenting than their 1960s confreres.

Fr Harrison found the "one single question in the survey which, more than any other, could be taken as a kind of rough litmus test of basic or overall orthodoxy" was the one which asked, "Do you think Roman Catholics must follow all of the Church's teachings to be faithful, or do you think they may disagree on some issues and still be considered faithful?".

Younger priests tended to agree with the first option while older priests preferred the second.

When the responses to 13 questions on doctrine were broken down according to the length of time respondents had been in the priesthood, it was found that priests ordained in the mid to late 1960s — and now mainly aged in their sixties — were, with remarkable consistency, the most "liberal" or dissenting of all age groups.

On the other hand, there was evidence of a movement back to orthodoxy among the "John Paul II priests" ordained in the last two decades.

This picture matched that in Australia. According to Melbourne's former Director of Vocations, Fr Paul Stuart, today's seminarians "are different in that they seem to have fewer problems with the authority of the Church".[8]

Queensland

The situation in Australia mirrors the American pattern.

Of all Australian states, Queensland — as far as the Catholic Church is concerned — has been the most consistently liberal since the Second Vatican Council. While significant changes have occurred elsewhere since the early 1990s, much of Queensland remains trapped in a late 1960s time-warp.

In 1990, Fr Frank Lourigan, then Rector of the Brisbane seminary which serves the five Queensland dioceses, offered an overview of the formation potential recruits could expect.[9]

A priest's "specific gift of ministry, the Sacrament of his ministry", he said, "was to give meaning to the many gifts of the communion of the faithful", to "recognise the action of the Spirit in the fresh movements among the human communities he is committed to serve" and to be "comfortable with the uncomfortability of the new human challenges — ecology, women's participation in society and Church, and in the search for effective and just economic and political systems for all humanity".

In Fr Lourigan's view, it was "the capacity to live with the ambiguity of a Church in transition that is most required of the priest today; to be able to live with a vision for something new and to work for it". This meant that many people would be "empowered to accept responsibility" and many new ministries would "flower in ways we have only dreamed about all this time".

This job description apparently failed to tempt many new recruits, with numbers at the seminary continuing to fall. In 1997, not one entered Brisbane's seminary for the academic year leaving the full complement for all year levels at 20. By 2006, according to reliable Brisbane sources, there would be a mere five or six seminarians (including one man in his 60s) for Queensland's five dioceses, at a time when the state's population has soared above four million, twice the 1976 population, and Brisbane is Australia's fastest growing archdiocese, with 1,000 to 1,500 arriving every week.[10]

The then Rector, Fr John Chalmers, was reported as saying in 1997 that the zero intake was "not a cause for alarm" as at the same time there were more than 100 people registered for theological study and "many of those could opt to enter the ordination program later". Evidently not, to judge from the above figures.

In 2005, coinciding with Vocations Week, from 7-14 August, came release of "A Pastoral Letter of the Bishops of Queensland on Vocations to the Priesthood",[11] as well as an "Open Letter to the Priests of Queensland" from Father Michael McCarthy, then Rector of the Holy Spirit Seminary in Brisbane.[12]

In their Pastoral Letter, the bishops spelled out the seriousness of the situation. "In some ways", they said, "we need to start again, to rebuild the priesthood of the Queensland Church. There is a gap in age and formation needing to be bridged between the majority of priests who are working in our parishes and those whom we believe Christ is calling and will continue to call in the future".

Fr McCarthy confirmed this concern. "There are", he said, "currently nine men in the Holy Spirit Seminary at various stages of their formation and we are hopeful of more joining the Seminary in the near future". In fact, by 2006, as indicated, Queensland's seminary numbers would decline further.

The above Pastoral Letter foreshadowed changes in the seminary program. "The Bishops of Queensland", it said, "are working towards a new future for the priesthood by reconfiguring the Holy Spirit Seminary and its formation program and the educational program offered by St Paul's Theological College".

In June 2006, the Queensland bishops announced that a new seminary would be built on the Banyo site, now largely occupied by a campus of Australian Catholic University. Whether this "reconfiguration" would bring about a much-needed increase in seminarians remained to be seen.

Wagga Wagga

A historical moment for Australia's seminaries took place in 1992 with the official opening of the new Vianney College seminary in the small NSW Diocese of Wagga Wagga (present Catholic population about 65,000) on 29 March. Two years later, additions would be needed when the seminary intake exceeded capacity.

This was the bold initiative of Bishop William Brennan. He was fortified by the knowledge that when Cardinal Ratzinger became Archbishop of Munich he too founded a local seminary to provide suitable formation for seminarians.

Previously, Wagga Wagga's seminarians had studied in Sydney where, as with the rest of Australia's seminaries, the "spirit of Vatican II" still reigned supreme.

While Bishop Brennan — understandably — did not point to Sydney's deficiencies as the reason for his initiative, emphasising instead the particular needs of a rural diocese, it was clear he intended his future priests to have an orthodox formation and education. His seminary program would actually anticipate the thrust of John Paul II's Apostolic Exhortation on the Priesthood, *Pastores Dabo Vobis*.

The present Vianney College Rector, Fr Peter Thompson CM, described the founding of Vianney College "as the beginning of a process of reform that has been taken up by other seminaries".[13]

Fr Thompson said that while his visits to other seminaries gave him "some valuable insights into formation of priests which I have introduced here", he "also noted that many of the reforms I witnessed have been part of our policy from the beginning".

Many of Wagga Wagga's earlier intakes had come from dioceses where the seminaries were in poor shape, with Wagga Wagga seen as the only orthodox option available. When reforms took place in these seminaries, there was less need to train in Wagga Wagga.

While Wagga Wagga's enrolment of twelve in 2006 (eleven for Wagga Wagga and one for Armidale Diocese) was down from its peak figure of 24 seminarians in 1997, it was still the highest in Australia as a ratio of seminarians to Catholic population.

Thanks to Bishop Brennan's unswerving faith, tenacity and foresight, however, by 2004 there were 25 priests, most of them serving in Wagga Wagga, who had done all or some of their training at Vianney College. As a result the diocese has the youngest average age for its clergy and the best ratio of priests to Catholic population in Australia.

The present bishop of Wagga Wagga, Bishop Gerard Hanna, has indicated the seminary will continue as long as its numbers make it viable.

In 2004, a retreat day held at the seminary for single men interested in discerning a vocation attracted 26. A similar retreat conducted by the Confraternity of Christ the Priest, a community of priests and brothers within the diocese, was just as successful. Fr Thompson saw these as hopeful signs along with "the team of capable and orthodox lecturers that are available to teach in Vianney College".

Perth

In the Archdiocese of Perth, a similar process has occurred since the advent of Archbishop Barry Hickey. Beginning in 1994, Perth would have its own major seminary of St Charles in Guildford. Previously its students had completed their studies in Adelaide.[14]

Since then, seminary numbers have gradually increased making Perth the most successful archdiocese in Australia on a seminarian per Catholic population basis.

In 1998, Archbishop Hickey offered an explanation for this success. "The response of young men to the priesthood has much to do with their understanding of what the priesthood is all about", he said.

"A 'low theology' of priesthood, that is, one which speaks of the 'ordained ministry' as one ministry among many, one which would eliminate all 'distinctions' of dress, title and distinctive way of life, attracts very few.

"A 'high theology' of priesthood which speaks of the sacramental identification with the priesthood of Jesus Christ, and the call to be 'another Christ' for people, together with outward signs of this inner consciousness by way of dress and lifestyle, remains attractive.

"Perhaps we see in this distinction a way of attracting more vocations to the diocesan priesthood.

"This year, six men will be ordained to the priesthood for the Archdiocese of Perth, five of whom will be ordained in Perth, and one in Rome.

"All of them wish to be 'other Christs' to their people, and identify with the 'high theology' of the priesthood contained in the papal documents, especially in *Pastores Dabo Vobis*, issued by the present Holy Father in 1992".

By 2000 the total number of ordinations had increased to fourteen.[15]

This increase was due to the fact that Archbishop Hickey had set up a second seminary, Redemptoris Mater, run by priests associated with the Neo-Catechumenate. Its students generally do not come from Perth but from Neo-Catechumenal groups around the world. When ordained, they serve in the archdiocese for a few years before leaving for overseas postings.

Commenting on the increasing seminary numbers, Archbishop Hickey said, "We consciously resist the modern tendency to minimise the difference between the ministerial priesthood of Holy Orders and the universal priesthood of Baptism because to do so affects vocations.

Unless young men can see there is a real difference between the two, the call to Holy Orders is not clearly made or heard".

The Archbishop summed up his approach as follows.

• Create a real desire for priestly vocations at all levels in the Church: among priests, parishes, schools, prayer groups and movements and in tertiary institutions.

• Aim high. Despite public scandals, or perhaps even because of them, the unique dignity of the priesthood should be stressed. This has a powerful appeal for those wishing to give themselves totally to the Lord.

• Do not hope or expect that married clergy will be the answer. Celibacy is not a barrier. It is part of the lofty ideal that attracts.

• Avoid terms like 'the ordained ministry' that minimise the difference between the priesthood of Holy Orders and the universal priesthood of Baptism.

• Select seminary staff that share this vision and who are themselves good models of priestly dedication and spirituality.

• Accept students from other countries (also priests) with careful screening.

• Base one's theology of the priesthood on papal documents, not on theological speculation.

The ordination of nine men to the priesthood in Perth's St Mary's Cathedral in December 2005

• Pray and expect vocations to come. If we believe Jesus is calling sufficient numbers to the priesthood, we must never give in to negativity or be inhibited by those who are opposed to priestly ordinations for whatever reason.

Melbourne

In late 1996, just a few months after the appointment of Archbishop George Pell, all the Bishops of Victoria and Tasmania agreed there should be a different type of religious formation at the Corpus Christi Seminary from the one used previously.

The proposed reforms, which were due to begin in 1997, were based on *Pastores Dabo Vobis* and included increased periods of retreat, changes to daily devotions, more meditation and recollection and a more intensive study of the Church's forms of public worship.

This decision sparked a mass resignation by the seminary staff with the Rector, Fr Paul Connell, indicating to the Melbourne *Herald Sun* that the staff were not willing to run the seminary in a "new style". One of the departing staff members was quoted as saying the proposals were a "subtle vote of no confidence" in the existing administration and its operations, and that the move to a "stricter and more regulatory regime was not welcomed by the staff".[16]

Archbishop Pell's response was to accept the resignations and appoint a new seminary staff more attuned to the thinking of John Paul II.

Meanwhile, priests in two of Victoria's regional dioceses were quick to voice their opposition.[17]

In Ballarat, a meeting of the Council of Priests was highly critical of the reforms as the meeting's minutes reveal. One response read: "If the Archbishop of Melbourne can 'railroad' through changes at the seminary, where will it stop? Are we in a position to do anything?" and "[It] appears that the Archbishop of Melbourne is now running the Victorian and Tasmanian Church".

Concern was expressed about the "sort of theology" that might be taught at Corpus Christi and it was asked "What kind of person will now want to enter the seminary?" Suggested solutions to this included "a preparatory program in the diocese" for Ballarat's students "before they go to the seminary" or even "options for our students other than the seminary". One priest asked "Should an alternative be found for Ballarat seminary students?"

A motion was then carried unanimously: "That the Council of

Seminarians at Corpus Christi in Melbourne

Priests recommends that the Bishop set up a body of competent people in the Diocese to review the priestly formation needs of the Diocese and report to the Bishop with recommendations by July 1997 considering:

• the special needs of rural clergy,

• a future of collaborative ministry;

• the on-going life-long nature of human, spiritual and professional formation of priests in ministry and being open to draw on the theological resources within the Province or wider, as required".

Since at the end of 1996 there was just one student for the Ballarat Diocese at the Corpus Christi seminary (and still just one in 2006), these concerns were purely academic.

This state of affairs was underlined by an earlier report in the minutes from the Vocations Committee which stated that a "Day of Discovery" scheduled for several regional centres had been "cancelled due to [the] very small interest shown". The solitary Day of Discovery held in Horsham drew just five people. No doubt the Ballarat Council of Priests asked themselves why so few were interested.

Similar concerns were voiced at a meeting of the Council of Priests of the Victorian Diocese of Sale.

In 1998, Archbishop Pell relocated the Corpus Christi Seminary from the distant suburb of Clayton to inner-city Carlton, close to St Patrick's Cathedral, with an old gothic-style bluestone church restored to its original condition as the seminary's chapel. The new site contrasted markedly with the soulless seminary buildings in Clayton, known by its orthodox critics as "Clayton Place".[18]

In 1999, Melbourne's new Vocations Director, Fr Paul Stuart, set out the fresh thinking that would be guiding the reformed seminary:[19] "Dioceses, religious orders, religious movements and prayer groups that attract and keep vocations and members do not have new methods, new courses, new discoveries, a new magic formula or a new Church. They have old but radical ones, and they have been at the service of the Holy Spirit for millennia. See them, if you will, in the lives and initiatives of the great founders of the religious congregations and Catholic associations, old and new.

"I have great hope in the springtime that Pope John Paul II is shepherding us towards. The youth, in varying momentum around the world, are responding to the call to holiness and Christian service. As useful and beneficial as clever vocational advertisements and promotions are, nothing will beat or replace the example of Christ himself and those who imitate him in their lives, in their priesthood, marriage, family, work and vocation.

"Promote Christ and you promote vocations — he is the priest, spouse and servant exemplar.

"Promote prayer, penance, Eucharistic and Marian devotion, fidelity and unity on matters of faith and morality, Christian service, and you sow seeds in the vineyard that not even the weeds of the culture of death, the sceptics, the cynics and the evil-doers can strangle".

The reforms set in motion by Archbishop Pell were soon bearing fruit with an increase in seminary numbers from 12 in 1996 to 31 in 2002 for the Melbourne Archdiocese.[20]

However, the figures have remained miniscule for the other Victorian dioceses and Tasmania, with the exception of Sandhurst, which had five in the seminary in 2005, thanks to the vigorous promotion of vocations by Bishop Joseph Grech.

Sydney

Since his appointment to Sydney in 2001, Archbishop (now Cardinal) George Pell has given priestly vocations top priority and his full support. Numbers have been steadily increasing since 2001, with around 40 in the seminary in 2003.[21]

Fr Julian Porteous was appointed as Rector of the Seminary of the Good Shepherd, Strathfield, which trains future priests for the Sydney Archdiocese as well as for other NSW dioceses.

After his first twelve months as Rector, Fr Porteous (now Bishop Porteous) offered some thoughts on what he saw as "a new type of seminarian", compared with his own late-1960s experience.

Today's seminarians, he said, "enter at a later age, often the mid-20s and beyond (a number are in their 40s)" and come from smaller family units.

Some of these vocations "appear not so much to emerge from a general solid Catholic culture fostered in home, parish and school, but rather out of a personal conviction of faith akin to conversion" being a "post-postmodern" generation, "who have embraced a Catholicism that provides a solid grounding and focus for their lives in the midst of a relativised ethical and social culture experienced in the world around them".

As Fr Porteous put it, "They look particularly to Pope John Paul II, the only pope they have ever known, as representing what they seek from the Church — strong and courageous ideals, a countercultural ethical position, and a strongly transcendental vision of faith".

Fr Porteous referred to *Pastores Dabo Vobis*, in which John Paul II said a priest must be "humanly as credible and acceptable as possible". The Sydney seminary had responded with focus on the formation of Christian character by drawing on classical Catholic teaching on the virtues, especially those that are particularly priestly, special emphasis being given to the charism of celibacy.

The Rector also referred to a document from the Congregation for the Clergy (August 2002) that sought, among other things, to clarify the distinction between the common priesthood of the faithful and the ministerial priesthood, as one "not only in grade but also in essence" and the need to overcome what is now being identified as "the clericalising of the laity and the secularising of the clergy".

During an interview with this writer in 2006, Bishop Porteous observed that today's seminarians are "really interested in a solid Catholic faith and spirituality" and "strongly attracted to clear expressions of Catholic identity".

He explained further, "I am concerned with the state of society. It has changed much since I was in the seminary. The ravages of secularism are great indeed. We face a crisis of truth and a crisis of faith. The crisis of truth — the result of post-modernism — has led to a new generation of young people who desperately seek what is solid and irrefutable. They want to base their lives on rock".

This is reflected in the solid formation provided at the Sydney Seminary, with its daily Rule of Life including celebration of the Divine Office in common in the chapel for morning, evening and night prayers, along with daily Mass. A half hour of meditation is scheduled after morning prayer and is held in the chapel in common.

Three-quarters of an hour of Eucharistic Adoration takes place every night and an hour of Eucharistic Adoration each Sunday afternoon.

An Annual Retreat is held for the whole seminary community and Days of Reflection are set aside during the semester for the community to spend a time in prayer or recollection. Seminarians are also expected to make a regular confession.

Silence is required after 10:30pm until after morning Mass the next day and all conversations, phone calls, and TV watching have to stop by 10:30pm, with any visitors leaving by then. There is also a clearly defined dress code for the seminarians.

Regarding academic formation, which occurs at the Catholic Institute of Sydney, Bishop Porteous has pointedly told the Institute he expects it to be one which "nurtures and inspires the personal faith of the seminarian — faith seeking understanding" and "presents unambiguously the truth of the Catholic Church captured in the Scriptures and the Tradition".

This, he believes, will produce seminarians "who are soaked in the Word of God as a living word", who have "formed a Catholic mind" and who "have a heightened moral conscience and a firm grasp of Catholic moral teaching".

Seminarians at prayer in Sydney's Good Shepherd Seminary chapel

Bishop Porteous makes clear that as Rector his principal objective is "to produce good and holy priests".

"A priest", he says, "stands in the midst of the secular culture of our day as a man set apart. He no longer belongs to the common run of people, even of Christians. He is a priest in their midst. He is a man of God. He belongs not to this world, but to the reign of God.

"As a priest he will be a sign of contradiction, and at times a subject of persecution or rejection. He will be a mystery to many. He will be a reminder of the Divine to others preoccupied with the present".

Current seminary numbers

The steady increases at most Australian seminaries since the 1990s reforms began have continued. Following their low points of recruitment, intakes in both Melbourne and Sydney have risen steadily, as elsewhere.[22]

In Sydney, there were 44 students in residence in 2006, the largest number since the earlier decline set in and double the number five years earlier when Archbishop Pell was appointed to Sydney. In addition, there are three seminarians studying in Rome.

Overall, 30 of the 44 seminarians are attached to the Sydney Archdiocese, with three for Adelaide, two each for Lismore and Canberra-Goulburn, and one each for Woolongong and Broome (WA). There are also three training for dioceses in Burma and two for Uganda.

The recently established Redemptoris Mater Sydney (or Archdiocesan Missionary seminary), operated by the Neocatechumenate as in Perth, with 50 missionary seminaries worldwide, had 18 seminarians in residence for 2006. On ordination, its priests will serve for several years in the Sydney Archdiocese before being assigned to other parts of the world.

The other two dioceses covering parts of the Sydney metropolitan area are Parramatta and Broken Bay. Parramatta has its own arrangements and does not send candidates to the Good Shepherd Seminary. The Diocese of Broken Bay, which normally sends them there, has had few if any seminarians for several years.

In Perth, the St Charles Seminary had 20 students for 2006, following nine ordinations for the Perth Archdiocese in 2005. Of the 20 students, fifteen were for Perth, four for Geraldton and one for Bunbury. The Neocatechumenate's Redemptoris Mater Seminary had 20 students for 2006. Overall, since Archbishop Hickey took over in 1991, there have been 81 ordinations.

In Melbourne, numbers continued to increase, with ten new seminarians entering in 2005 — all for the Melbourne Archdiocese. Of the total of 41 seminarians at Corpus Christi in 2006, 30 were for the Melbourne Archdiocese, three each for Vietnam and for the Sandhurst Diocese, one each for Ballarat, Sale and Bathurst (NSW) and none for Tasmania — a state which seems to be leading the rest of Australia towards priestlessness.

The seminary situation in Queensland stands in stark contrast to the steady growth elsewhere, with, as noted earlier, its 2006 total of five or six for all five dioceses, or about half the number of seminarians in the small diocese of Wagga Wagga.

According to the 2006/2007 *Official Directory of the Catholic Church in Australia*, there were 44 in formation for the religious priesthood across Australia in 2005 — covering about 40 different orders.

However, the small Priestly Fraternity of St Peter, which celebrates the classical Latin Liturgy, had five students for the priesthood in 2005 and a presence in Melbourne, Sydney, Parramatta and Canberra.

Endnotes

1. Zenit News Service, May 2006.
2. Fr Timothy Deeter, "Many vocations, empty seminaries", *Medjugorje Magazine*, October 1994.
3. "US Bishop solves the vocations crisis", *AD2000*, July 1993, p. 4.
4. Michael Rose, *Priests: Portraits of Ten Good Men Serving the Church Today*, Sophia Institute Press, Manchester, NH, 2003.
5. *Catholic World Report*, July 2005.
6. Carter H. Griffin, *Homiletic & Pastoral Review*, October 2004.
7. Fr Brian W. Harrison OS, "The Clergy and the Culture Wars", *Culture Wars*, February 2003, pp. 6-19.
8. "Australian diocesan seminary numbers continue to increase". *AD2000*, March 2005, p. 3.
9. *The Catholic Leader* (Brisbane), 16 September 1990.

10. Michael Gilchrist, "Where zero recruits is not a cause for alarm", *AD2000*, March 1997, pp. 5-6.
11. *A Pastoral Letter of the Bishops of Queensland on Vocations to the Priesthood*, Vocations Week, 7-14 August 2005.
12. Fr Michael McCarthy, "Open Letter to the Priests of Queensland", Holy Spirit Seminary, Brisbane, August 2005.
13. Fr Peter Thompson CM, Rector, Vianney College, Wagga Wagga, NSW, "Seminary reforms", *AD2000*, December 2004-January 2005, p. 14.
14. "A new major seminary for Perth", *AD2000*, December 1993-January 1994, p. 9.
15. Archbishop Barry Hickey, "Perth's priestly vocations success story", *AD2000*, August 2000, pp. 3-4.
16. "Pell's priests quit", *Herald Sun* (Melbourne), 17 November 1996, p. 3.
17. "Local opposition to Corpus Christi Seminary reforms", *AD2000*, March 1997, p. 6.
18. "Seminary's new home", *Herald Sun*, 30 July 1998, p. 28.
19. Fr Paul Stuart, Vocations Director, Archdiocese of Melbourne, "Confronting today's vocations crisis", *AD2000*, May 1999, p. 3.
20. "Corpus Christi enrolments bounce back", *AD2000*, September 2002, p. 6.
21. Fr Julian Porteous, Rector, Good Shepherd Seminary, Sydney, "Sydney Seminary growth based on orthodoxy, fidelity", *AD2000*, February 2003, pp. 3-4.
22. Based on my discussions with seminary rectors and vocations directors in February 2005 and in May 2006.

Chapter Eleven

The Way Ahead

Australian Catholicism is declining in the key indicators of belief and practice and this will continue until the causes are addressed. The Church's Catholic identity faces a challenge of survival and time is running out if there is to be any overall spiritual recovery.

The factors making it possible for new generations to be formed into practising Catholics to an even moderate extent no longer exist, leaving only scattered pockets where a self-perpetuating Catholic culture exists. Practising parents, teachers, role models and peers are normally a minimum requirement for reinforcing the normalcy of Catholic orthodoxy — a rare combination these days.

In the current cultural climate of secularism and relativism which impacts on Catholics daily through the mass media, movies, advertising, the Internet, popular music, school curricula, universities and government, even these factors do not ensure long term practice. But they offer a much greater likelihood.

In the absence of these, there will be almost certain loss of faith, or at best a thin veneer of cafeteria Catholicism.

After almost 40 years, the "spirit of Vatican II" has had its day and failed comprehensively to deliver. Not only has it aggravated the impact of secularism on the Catholic community, it has had no long term drawing power among the young. Rock Masses and trendy catechetics may have had passing appeal, but young people soon sought their entertainment elsewhere, departing in droves, rarely if ever to return.

While few of today's school leavers are interested in religion, the only form of Catholicism capable of attracting these few is clear, unequivocal orthodoxy, as articulated by John Paul II and Benedict XVI. Lukewarm accommodation with secularism is a recipe for gradual spiritual death, as is occurring with other mainline Christian denominations that have long been kneeling before the world.

In the Universal Church's Queensland Branch, already a religious basket case, if a rapid turnaround is not initiated within five years — at the outside — the faith will have all but evaporated in Australia's soon-to-be second largest state in population.

The signs are there — six parishes in Brisbane are now under one priest, deaneries of 11 or 12 parishes have only one or two priests under 65 and churches are closing. The concerned faithful simply do not know where to turn.

A similar situation prevails in other "spirit of Vatican II" dioceses that are failing to attract priestly vocations.

Overview

Today, most of the Church's educational institutions are no longer able or prepared to fulfil their essential task of forming future practising Catholics. In many cases they effectively erase what little faith is left.

The following facts identified in earlier chapters confirm this:

• There are few if any differences in belief and practice between State school-educated and Catholic school-educated Catholics. Many Catholic parents now send their children to the better State schools or non-Catholic independent schools while doing their own catechising — usually with better results for their children's practice of the faith.

• Regular Mass attendance (at least 2-3 times per month) is now barely five per cent for Catholic school leavers, and similar for Catholics in their 20s. The national average of 15 per cent (or 13 per cent weekly attendance) as of 2001 — if present trends continue — is likely to decline towards five percent in the coming decades as the older age groups depart.

• Most young Catholics training to be teachers in Catholic schools do not accept (or even know about) the Church's teachings, e.g., at Australian Catholic University, just one-third of undergraduates (many of them intending teachers) believed in the Real Presence in the Eucharist and only 14 per cent agreed with the Church's teaching on abortion.

• There is little difference in beliefs and practices between first year and final year students at the Australian Catholic University which trains the largest number of Catholic teachers in Australia.

• Most teachers and principals in Catholic schools no longer subscribe to all the Church's teachings.

• Only a small minority of Catholic parents and students are concerned about the specifically Catholic dimension of Catholic schools.

• In moral areas such as premarital sex, contraception, abortion, divorce and remarriage, there is a low level of acceptance of the Church's teachings even among regular Mass-goers. As a whole, the Catholic community differs little if at all from the rest of the Australian population on these and other moral issues.

Today, the Catholic school system in general is no longer capable of delivering. Even with the best will in the world and the best religion texts, their task is almost impossible when few parents practise the faith. In many Catholic secondary schools, negative peer group pressure tends to finish off any vestige of religious commitment.

Parish life in parts of Australia is dying, either through being priest-less, bereft of parishioners, or a combination of both. Parish visitations by priests are almost a thing of the past and even the older "pre-Vatican II" Catholics are falling away from practice of the faith with less than a third of them attending Mass regularly.

It is not surprising, given this situation, that there is such a widespread paralysis of leadership. Many of the bishops seem more like helpless spectators at the Church's steady decline, if they are not already part of the problem.

Lesson from history

The situation in 19th century France which the famous Curé d'Ars (St John Vianney) encountered in his parish was, in miniature, not unlike what today's bishops face across Australia. What he did to address the crisis of faith in his time may point the way for our Church leaders.

The Curé arrived at his parish a generation after unparalleled cultural and political upheaval following the French Revolution and the rule of Napoleon. Secularism dominated much of French society, with even the smaller villages feeling its impact. God and the Church were shunted more and more to the margins of French life.

Religious ignorance and indifference were common among children and adults in Ars with people frequently missing Sunday Mass. But there were still scattered remnants of faithful Catholicism to be found among a few of the village's families.

The Curé's pastoral strategy had eight basic features: his own personal sanctity; being approachable and receptive to others; prayer and ascetical living; concentrating on those families still practising; giving special attention to the liturgy, preaching and catechesis; addressing problems at their roots and not in their symptoms; planting good habits of prayer and works of mercy; and doing it all with a strong priestly identity.

He first focused on the families that were strong in their faith and had resisted the waves of worldliness and indifference. He saw them as becoming the fiery coals, which would dry out the damp wood of the rest of the parish and help set it ablaze. His work had a ripple effect expanding outward from these initial families to more and more of the village and surrounding area.

Since people were not coming to Mass on Sundays, he began to beautify the parish church, making it attractive to people. The place of the Eucharist was to be a place of beauty. He even used his own money to purchase a new altar and statuary.

His preaching was clear and focused on the central mysteries of the faith, including the prospect of Hell for unrepentant sinners and the need for reconciliation with God through confession. He worked hard preparing his sermons through hours of study each week.

What St John Vianney did with eventual success on a small scale suggests the most realistic approach to today's problems.

Communities of faith

The situation today, following the late 1960s cultural revolution and years of "spirit of Vatican II" misinformation and confusion is not unlike what the Curé d'Ars encountered, with most Australian Catholics ignorant, careless, apathetic or hostile regarding Church teachings.

But many small communities, groups and families remain strong in their faith and possess the necessary elements for maintaining commitment and forming new generations of practising Catholics.

Here and there, we find priests in parishes who evangelise enthusiastically and celebrate the Mass reverently, schools and colleges with a strong concentration of practising parents and teachers, such as Tangara and Redfield in Sydney, groups attending Latin Masses, home schoolers, faithful communities of religious, organisations of clergy, religious, university students and professionals with a love of the Catholic faith and some of the more religiously devout ethnic groups— especially the Asian Australians — whose family life is still strong.

Internationally, the new movements such as Communion and Liberation, Focolare, Neocatechumenal Way, Opus Dei, San Egidio Community and the charismatic movements have been effective evangelisers of their members and the seedbeds of religious and priestly vocations.

Bishops need to support and encourage the orthodox faithful, ensuring their continuing fidelity and growth. Each group or community is capable of the ripple effect that St John Vianney achieved.

The easier availability of Eternal Word Television Network (EWTN) in Australia means that a well-presented orthodox message can reach even the most isolated Catholics and reinforce the new evangelisation among families. Bishops need to give the expansion of EWTN their complete backing.

Catholic education

Elsewhere, as both John Paul II and Benedict XVI have indicated, those parts of the Church no longer meriting the label Catholic should have it withdrawn. Scarce resources should not be wasted on unproductive sources of spiritual infection and confusion.

One area calling for urgent surgery is Catholic education.

Re-establishing a Catholic identity in even a few schools and colleges would require fundamental reform involving a back to the drawing boards approach.

An ideal — but clearly impossible — solution would be for the Church to sell off all of its schools, colleges, CEOs and the Australian Catholic University to the highest bidders and start again from scratch.

At present, practising teachers, parents and students — a small minority of the total — are scattered around a large number of schools in each diocese. These people need to be concentrated in fewer schools so that the faith of all concerned is mutually reinforced instead of eroded by non-practising majorities as is often the case now.

This process could be started by groups of like-minded parents and teachers co-operating in setting up small schools. Sympathetic bishops ought encourage such moves through their public approval, promotion and provision of diocesan facilities. Otherwise bishops might take the initiative by setting up, for example, an excellence award for schools willing and able to meet certain essential criteria of Catholicity. Either way, they may need to bypass their educational bureaucrats.

Teaching staffs would need to be practising Catholics, with a commitment to Church teachings made in writing (as is required of educators in some American dioceses). Parents wishing to enrol their children in an "award" school would be asked to make a similar commitment, including a pledge to co-operate with the spiritual work of the school.

An award school's religion courses would be monitored to ensure that the Church's doctrinal and moral teachings are given full and adequate coverage at the appropriate year levels. Students' knowledge and understanding of the faith would be tested regularly, with periodic inspections of the schools to confirm their award status.

School Masses would follow the Church's liturgical requirements with provision made for students' spiritual needs, such as Eucharistic adoration, confessions, rosaries, prayers before and after classses and an orthodox chaplain. Practical Christianity through various works of charity would be another priority.

The diocese should publicise the fact that particular schools had met the criteria so parents seeking an authentic Catholic education for their children could apply to one of them.

Over time, practising Catholic teachers and parents would gravitate towards award schools, causing overflows and the need for new ones to be set up. In large centres like Melbourne and Sydney, enough schools might eventually qualify so that there would be coverage of metropolitan areas and reasonable access for any interested parents. This process would be more difficult in the sparsely populated outback dioceses where the necessary human resources are spread far more thinly.

Bishops might also compile a register of parishes, religious communities, organisations and assorted enterprises that merit the label Catholic. Catholics looking for reinforcement of their faith could select from a range of options.

This approach would at least help consolidate the Catholic remnants and give them a chance of survival and future growth. Over time, they might produce small "ripples" here and there that touch the rest of the Catholic population.

If things are left as they are, the ripple effect will continue to work in reverse, with the remnants themselves being gradually eroded by the non-practising majority as well as by the secular culture.

Broader approach

The bottom line for any broader turnaround, along with a more active role by orthodox lay people, is strong episcopal leadership in every diocese. This could be a tall order in the short term, with many ineffectual bishops — paralysed by fear of offending the secular media, or worse, their powerful bureaucracies — still years away from retirement.

It would be encouraging if the bishops of Australia as a body (or more likely individually) launched a well-publicised program of perpetual adoration in cathedrals and parishes and encouraged Catholics to participate. This would be a dramatic challenge for the faithful to stand and be counted on the bottom line doctrine — the Real Presence in the Eucharist. Some of the previously indifferent might respond.

Individual confessions should be made available at convenient times before and after Masses, and during perpetual adoration. The option of anonymity would make it easier for Catholics who have slipped away from practice of the faith over many years to approach the confessional.

More effective campaigns to promote priestly and religious vocations could also be linked with perpetual adoration.

The over-use of lay people as helpers or substitutes for priests in the liturgy should be wound back as this has had the effect of weakening awareness of the essential role of priests and discouraging vocations. The excessive and often unwarranted use of Extraordinary Ministers of Holy Communion ("special ministers") must be brought to an end. These should be rare exceptions rather than the rule.

Like the Curé d'Ars, bishops need to encourage beauty and a sense of the sacred in the liturgy throughout their dioceses. This would be linked to the fostering of choirs, suitable sacred music and greater reverence in churches.

The younger priests emerging from reformed seminaries are an important means of achieving these ends as well as connecting with the unchurched in parishes — as some are already doing to good effect. Although they are relatively few in number, it has been a start.

The time for denial, compromise, half-measures, diplomacy, distractions and pious hope is over. If the Church in Australia is to have any long term future with its integrity intact, bishops have to give maximum support to orthodoxy everywhere in practical ways without fear or favour, including firm action against theological dissent and liturgical abuses as called for by the *Statement of Conclusions*. The usual suspects will be outraged but this is to be expected and has to be worn — even when the secular media get involved.

The "signs of the times" today call for consolidation of a Catholic identity and sifting the wheat from the chaff. This will require particularly strong leadership.

Bishops unable or unwilling to follow such a tough but necessary course should submit their resignations — the sooner the better — and make way for those who can. In future only candidates equal to the task should be appointed — meaning that the present selection process will have to be tightened up.

Australia could well be a test case for the rest of the Western world where the Christian churches, as Benedict XVI believes, are dying. If Catholicism in Australia can meet the challenge of survival, where the position is among the worst, there might be hope and, indeed, inspiration for the rest.

But time is running out for any general turning of the tide.

Index